INSPIRATIONAL
AND MOTIVATIONAL
SHORT STORIES

128 Inspiring Stories with
Life Changing Wisdom to Live By

Compiled by Barry Phillips

Published by
Filament Publishing Ltd
16 Croydon Road, Beddington
Croydon, Surrey, CR0 4PA, United Kingdom
www.filamentpublishing.com
Telephone: +44 (0)208 688 2598

Inspirational And Motivational Stories
by Barry Phillips
© 2019 Barry Phillips
ISBN 978-1-912635-66-5
Printed by IngramSpark

TABLE OF CONTENTS

THE BOOK
AND ITS AUTHOR

For more than two decades I have run a company in the self-development arena that has sold over one million books. In that time, I have collected quotes and stories that captured my attention. In 2013 I published my first book "Life Changing Quotes" which has gone on to be an Amazon bestseller. Around the same time the company started a monthly blog aimed at sharing some of these life changing stories called "Something to Think About". The response was amazing, and people loved how they made them feel. Some of the stories in this book were originally in those blogs; I hope they will make you laugh, cry and, ultimately, give you all something to think about.

There are many treasures to unearth in this book. Wherever you are on your own path, these short stories and poems will assist you in your journey to peace and contentment. Pay them close attention, and let them talk to the depths of your being.

And, if you are a parent, a speaker, coach, teacher or business owner, you'll find this publication to be an invaluable resource whenever you want to illustrate a point by telling a story.

Some of them are easy to understand, others need more time to ponder; but all of them are profoundly meaningful.

When life gets tough, a simple, well-told story or metaphor can help us look at a situation with new eyes. The distilled essence of how a character in a story copes with the challenges of life can teach us an important lesson. For a short moment, a story helps to quieten our mind, allowing us to take a deep breath and regain some serenity. In this sense, a good, powerful story can act as a wise, compassionate guide.

These stories and poems have inspired and motivated me to live my life with more purpose and passion; many have profoundly impacted my life. Take the time to discover the possible meanings for your life.

I have attributed every story I could to the original source.

CHAPTER ONE : ACCEPTANCE

THE TATTOOED HOMELESS MAN

He was scary. He sat on the grass with his cardboard sign, his dog (actually his dog was adorable) and tattoos running up and down both arms and even on his neck. His sign proclaimed him to be "stuck and hungry" and to please help.

I'm a sucker for anyone needing help. My husband both loves and hates this quality in me. It often makes him nervous, and I knew if he saw me right now, he'd be nervous. But he wasn't with me right now.

I pulled the van over and in my rear-view mirror, contemplated this man, tattoos and all. He was youngish, maybe forty. He wore one of those bandanas tied over his head, biker/pirate style. Anyone could see he was dirty and had a scraggly beard. But if you looked closer, you could see that he had neatly tucked in the black T-shirt, and his things were in a small, tidy bundle. Nobody was stopping for him. I could see the other drivers take one look and immediately focus on something else - anything else.

It was so hot outside. I could see in the man's very blue eyes how dejected and tired and worn-out he felt. The sweat was trickling down his face. As I sat with the air-conditioning blowing, I remembered the quote, "Never judge a book by its cover".

I reached down into my purse and extracted a ten-dollar bill. My twelve-year old son, Nick, knew right away what I was doing. "Can I take it to him, Mom?"

"Be careful, honey," I warned and handed him the money. I watched in the mirror as he rushed over to the man, and, with a shy smile, handed it to him. I saw the man, startled, stand up and take the money, putting it into his back pocket. "Good," I thought to myself, "now he will at least have a hot meal tonight." I felt satisfied, proud of myself. I had made a sacrifice and now I could go on with my errands.

When Nick got back into the car, he looked at me with sad, pleading eyes. "Mom, his dog looks so hot and the man is really nice." I knew I had to do more.

"Go back and tell him to stay there, that we will be back in fifteen minutes," I told Nick. He bounded out of the car and ran to tell the tattooed stranger. I could see the man was surprised, but nodded his agreement. From my car, my heart did a little flip-flop of excitement.

We then ran to the nearest store and bought our gifts carefully. "It can't be too heavy," I explained to the children. "He has to be able to carry it around with him." We finally settled on our purchases. A bag of "Ol' Roy" (I hoped it was good - it looked good enough for me to eat! How do they make dog food look that way?!); a flavoured chew-toy shaped like a bone; a water dish, bacon flavoured snacks (for the dog); two bottles of water (one for the dog, one for Mr. Tattoos) and some people snacks for the man.

We rushed back to the spot where we had left him, and there he was, still waiting. And still nobody else was stopping for him. With hands shaking, I grabbed our bags and climbed out of the car, all four of my children following me, each carrying gifts. As we walked up to him, I had a fleeting moment of fear, hoping he wasn't a serial killer.

I looked into his eyes and saw something that startled me and made me ashamed of my judgment. I saw tears. He was fighting like a little boy to hold back his tears. How long had it been since someone showed this man kindness? I told him I hoped it wasn't too heavy for him to carry and showed him what we had brought. He stood there, like a child at Christmas, and I felt like my small contributions were so inadequate. When I took out the water dish, he snatched it out of my hands as if it were solid gold and told me he had had no way to give his dog water. He gingerly set it down, filled it with the bottled water we brought, and stood up to look directly into my eyes. His were so blue, so intense and my own filled with tears as he said, "Ma'am, I don't know what to say." He then put both hands on his bandana-clad head and just started to cry. This man, this "scary" man, was so gentle, so sweet and so humble.

I smiled through my tears and said, "Don't say anything." Then I noticed the tattoo on his neck. It said, "Mama tried."

As we all piled into the van and drove away, he was on his knees, arms around his dog, kissing his nose and smiling. I waved cheerfully and then fully broke down in tears.

I have so much. My worries seem so trivial and petty now. I have a home, a loving husband, and four beautiful children. I have a bed. I wondered where he would sleep tonight.

My step-daughter, Brandie, turned to me and said in the sweetest little-girl voice, "I feel so good."

Although it seemed as if we had helped him, the man with the tattoos gave us a gift that I will never forget. He taught us that no matter what the outside looks like, inside each of us is a human being deserving of kindness, of compassion, of acceptance. He opened my heart.

By Susan Fahncke

■ ■ ■

PUPPIES FOR SALE

A sign above the shop read; "Puppies for Sale."

Signs like these have a way of grabbing the attention of the children. A small boy, upon seeing the sign, entered into the shop asking, "How much are you selling the puppies for?"

The store owner said, "Anywhere from £30 to £50."

The little boy removed all the money he had from his pocket. "I have £2.37," he said. "Can I please look at them?"

The shop owner smiled and whistled. From the kennel, five cute puppies ran out. One puppy was lagging considerably behind. Pointing at the dog the little boy asked, "What is wrong with that one?"

The shopkeeper explained, "The puppy's hip socket is missing. At least, that is what the vet said. It will never walk properly again."

The little boy cheered with excitement, "That is the puppy that I want to buy."

"You don't have to buy that dog. You can have it for free."

The little boy was upset. He looked up at the shop owner and said, "I don't want you to give him to me. That dog is of equal worth as the rest of the dogs. I'll give you £2.37 now, and 50 pence a month until I have him fully paid for."

The shopkeeper replied, "Are you sure you want this dog? It is never going to walk, run or play with you like the other puppies."

The little boy reached down and lifted his trouser leg to reveal his crippled left leg, supported by a big metal brace. He looked up at the shop owner and softly replied, "Well, I don't run so well myself, and the little puppy will need someone who understands!"

Adapted from various versions on the internet.

SMILE

I am a mother of three, (ages fourteen, twelve and three), and have recently completed my college degree. The last class I had to take was Sociology. The teacher was absolutely inspiring with qualities that I wish every human being had been graced with. Her last project of the term was called "Smile."

The class was asked to go out and smile at three people and document their reactions. I am a very friendly person and always smile at everyone and say hello anyway, so, I thought, this would be a piece of cake.

Soon after we were assigned the project, my husband, youngest son and I went out to McDonald's one crisp March morning. It was just our way of sharing special playtime with our son. We were standing in line, waiting to be served, when all of a sudden everyone around us began to back away, and then even my husband did.

I did not move an inch...an overwhelming feeling of panic welled up inside of me as I turned to see why they had moved.

As I turned around, I smelled a horrible, "dirty body" smell, and there, standing behind me, were two poor, homeless men. As I looked down at the short gentleman, close to me, he was "smiling". His beautiful sky-blue eyes were full of God's Light as he searched for acceptance. He said, "Good day" as he counted the few coins he had been clutching. The second man fumbled with his hands as he stood behind his friend. I realised the second man was mentally handicapped and the blue-eyed gentleman was his salvation.

I held my tears as I stood there with them. The young lady at the counter asked him what they wanted. He said, "Coffee is all, Miss," because that was all they could afford.

(If they wanted to sit in the restaurant and warm-up, they had to buy something. He just wanted to be warm).

Then I really felt it - the compulsion was so great I almost reached out and embraced the little man with the blue eyes. That is when I noticed all eyes in the restaurant were set on me, judging my every action. I smiled and asked the young lady behind the counter to give me two more breakfast meals on a separate tray. I then walked around the corner to the table that the men had chosen as a resting spot.

I put the tray on the table and laid my hand on the blue-eyed gentleman's cold hand. He looked up at me, with tears in his eyes and said, "Thank you." I leaned over, began to pat his hand and said, "I did not do this for you. God is here working through me to give you hope." I started to cry as I walked away to join my husband and son.

When I sat down, my husband smiled at me and said, "That is why God gave you to me, honey, to give me hope."

We held hands for a moment and at that time we knew that only because of the Grace that we had been given were we able to give. We are not churchgoers, but we are believers.

That day showed me the pure Light of God's sweet love.

I returned to college, on the last evening of class, with this story in hand. I turned in "my project" and the instructor read it. Then she looked up at me and said, "Can I share this?"

I slowly nodded as she got the attention of the class. She began to read and that is when I knew that we, as human beings and being part of God, share this need to heal people and be healed.

In my own way I had touched the people at McDonald's, my husband, son, instructor, and every soul that shared the classroom on the last night I spent as a college student. I graduated with one of the biggest lessons I would ever learn:

Unconditional Acceptance

Author Unknown

■ ■ ■

MASKS

Don't be fooled by the face I wear, for I wear a thousand masks, and none of them are me. Don't be fooled, for goodness sake, don't be fooled.

I give you the impression that I'm secure, that confidence is my name and coolness is my game, and that I need no one. But don't believe me.

Beneath dwells the real me in confusion, in aloneness, in fear. That's why I create a mask to hide behind, to shield me from the glance that knows, but such a glance is precisely my salvation.

That is, if it's followed by acceptance, if it's followed by love. It's the only thing that can liberate me from my own self-built prison walls. I'm afraid that deep down I'm nothing and that I'm just no good and that you will reject me.

18

And so begins the parade of masks. I idly chatter to you. I tell you everything that's really nothing and nothing of what's everything, of what's crying within me.

Please listen carefully and try to hear what I'm not saying. I'd really like to be genuine and spontaneous, and me. But you've got to help me. You've got to hold out your hand.

Each time you're kind and gentle, and encouraging, each time you try to understand because you really care, my heart begins to grow wings, feeble wings, but wings.

With your sensitivity and sympathy, and your power of understanding, you alone can release me from my shallow world of uncertainty.

It will not be easy for you. The nearer you approach me, the blinder I may strike back.

But I'm told that Love is stronger than strong walls, and in this lies my only hope.

Please try to beat down these walls with firm hands,

But gentle hands, for a child is very sensitive.

Who am I, you wonder. I am every man you meet, and also every woman that you meet,

And I am you, also.

Author Unknown

DON'T WE ALL

I was parked in front of the mall wiping off my car. I had just come from the car wash and was waiting for my wife to get out of work. Coming my way from across the parking lot was what society would consider a 'bum'. From the looks of him, he had no car, no home, no clean clothes, and no money. There are times when you feel generous but there are other times when you just don't want to be bothered. This was one of those 'don't want to be bothered' times.

"I hope he doesn't ask me for any money," I thought. He didn't.

He came and sat on the curb in front of the bus stop but he didn't look like he could have enough money to even ride the bus. After a few minutes he spoke.

"That's a very pretty car," he said.

He was ragged but he had an air of dignity around him. His scraggly blond beard keeps more than his face warm. I said, "Thanks," and continued wiping off my car.

He sat there quietly as I worked. The expected plea for money never came. As the silence between us widened, something inside said, "Ask him if he needs any help." I was sure that he would say "yes" but I held true to the inner voice.

"Do you need any help?" I asked.

He answered in three simple but profound words that I shall never forget. We often look for wisdom in great men and women. We expect it from those of higher learning and accomplishments. I expected nothing but an outstretched, grimy hand. He spoke the three words that shook me.

"Don't we all?" he said. I was feeling high and mighty, successful and important, above a bum in the street, until those three words hit me like a twelve-gauge shotgun.

Don't we all?

I needed help. Maybe not for bus fare or a place to sleep, but I needed help. I reached in my wallet and gave him not only enough for bus fare, but enough to get a warm meal and shelter for the day. Those three little words still ring true. No matter how much you have, no matter how much you have accomplished, you need help too. No matter how little you have, no matter how loaded you are with problems, even without money or a place to sleep, you can give help.

Even if it's just a compliment, you can give that. You never know when you may see someone that appears to have it all. They are waiting on you to give them what they don't have; a different perspective on life, a glimpse at something beautiful, a respite from daily chaos that only you, through a torn world, can see. Maybe the man was just a homeless stranger wandering the streets. Maybe he was more than that.

Maybe he was sent by a power that is great and wise, to minister to a soul too comfortable in themselves.

Maybe God looked down, called an Angel, dressed him like a bum, and then said, "Go minister to that man cleaning the car, that man needs help."

Don't we all?

Author Unknown

THE INVITATION

It doesn't interest me what you do for a living.
I want to know what you ache for,
And if you dare to dream of meeting
Your heart's longing.

It doesn't interest me how old you are.
I want to know if you will risk looking like a fool
For love, for your dream,
For the adventure of being alive.

It doesn't interest me what planets are squaring your moon.
I want to know if you have touched the centre of your
    own sorrow,
If you have been opened by life's betrayals,
Or have become shrivelled and closed from fear of
    further pain.

I want to know if you can sit with pain,
Mine or your own,
Without moving
To hide it, or fade it, or fix it.

I want to know if you can be with joy,
Mine or your own,
If you can dance with wildness and let the ecstasy fill
    you to the tips of your fingers and toes,
Without cautioning us to be careful, be realistic,
    to remember the limitations of being human.

It doesn't interest me if the story you are telling me is true.
I want to know if you can disappoint another to be true
    to yourself,
If you can bear the accusation of betrayal and not
    betray your own soul.
I want to know if you can be faithless and therefore
    be trustworthy.

I want to know if you can see beauty
Even when it is not pretty every day,
And if you can source your own life
From its presence.

I want to know if you can live with failure,
Yours and mine,
And still stand on the edge of a lake and shout to the
    silver of the full moon,
"Yes!"

It doesn't interest me to know where you live or how
    much money you have.
I want to know if you can get up after the night of
    grief and despair,
Weary and bruised to the bone,
And do what needs to be done for the children.

It doesn't interest me who you are, how you came to be here.
I want to know if you will stand
In the centre of the fire with me
And not shrink back.

It doesn't interest me where or what or with whom
    you have studied.
I want to know what sustains you
From the inside
When all else falls away.

I want to know if you can be alone
With yourself,
And if you truly like the company you keep
In the empty moments.

By Oriah Mountain Dreamer

CHAPTER TWO : APPRECIATION

THE MOST BEAUTIFUL FLOWER

The park bench was deserted as I sat down to read
Beneath the long, straggly branches of an old willow tree.
Disillusioned by life with good reason to frown,
For the world was intent on dragging me down.

And if that weren't enough to ruin my day,
A young boy out of breath approached me, all tired from play.
He stood right before me with his head tilted down
And said with great excitement, "Look what I found!"

In his hand was a flower, and what a pitiful sight
With its petals all worn - not enough rain, or too little light
Wanting him to take his dead flower and go off to play,
I faked a small smile and then shifted away.

But instead of retreating he sat next to my side
And placed the flower to his nose and declared with surprise,
"It sure smells pretty and it's beautiful too,
That's why I picked it; here, it's for you."

The weed before me was dying or dead
Not vibrant of colours, orange, yellow or red
But I knew I must take it, or he might never leave
So I reached for the flower, and replied, "Just what I need."

But instead of him placing the flower in my hand,
He held it mid-air without reason or plan
It was then that I noticed for the very first time
That weed-toting boy could not see: he was blind.

I heard my voice quiver, tears shone like the sun
As I thanked him for picking the very best one.
"You're welcome," he smiled, and then ran off to play,
Unaware of the impact he'd had on my day.

I sat there and wondered how he managed to see
A self-pitying woman beneath an old willow tree.
How did he know of my self-indulged plight?
Perhaps from his heart, he'd been blessed with true sight.

Through the eyes of a blind child, at last I could see
The problem was not with the world; the problem was me
And for all of those times I myself had been blind,
I vowed to see beauty, and appreciate every second
    that's mine.

And then I held that wilted flower up to my nose
And breathed in the fragrance of a beautiful rose
And smiled as that young boy, another weed in his hand,
About to change the life of an unsuspecting old man.

Author Unknown

A CHRISTMAS MIRACLE

A little boy and his grandmother came to see Santa at The Mayfair Mall in December 1997 in Wisconsin, USA. The child climbed up on Santa's lap, holding a picture of a little girl.

"Who is this?" asked Santa, smiling. "Your friend? Your sister?"

"Yes Santa," he replied, "My sister, Sarah, who is very sick," he said sadly.

Santa glanced over at the grandmother who was waiting nearby and saw her dabbing her eyes with a tissue.

"She wanted to come with me to see you, oh so very much, Santa!" the child exclaimed. "She misses you," he added softly.

Santa tried to be cheerful and encouraged a smile on the boy's face, asking him what he wanted Santa to bring him for Christmas. When they finished their visit, the grandmother came over to help the child off his lap and started to say something to Santa, but halted.

"What is it?" Santa asked, warmly.

"Well, I know it's really too much to ask you, Santa, but ...," the old woman began, shooing her grandson over to one of Santa's elves to collect the little gift, which Santa gave all his young visitors.

"The girl in the photograph... my grandaughter. Well, you see ... she has leukaemia and isn't expected to make it even through the holidays," she said through tear-filled eyes. "Is

27

there anyway, Santa, any possible way that you could come see Sarah? That's all she wants for Christmas - to see Santa."

Santa blinked and swallowed hard and told the woman to leave information with his elves as to where Sarah was, and he would see what he could do. Santa thought of little else the rest of that afternoon. He knew what he had to do. "What if it were MY child lying in that hospital bed, dying?" he thought, with a sinking heart. "This is the least I can do."

When Santa had finished with all the other children's visits that evening, he retrieved the name of the hospital where Sarah was staying from his helper. He asked Rick, the assistant location manager, how to get to Children's Hospital. "Why?" Rick asked, with a puzzled look on his face. Santa relayed to him the conversation with Sarah's grandmother earlier that day. "Come on...I'll take you there myself," Rick said softly. Rick drove them to the hospital and came inside with Santa. They found out which room Sarah was in. A pale Rick said he would wait out in the hall.

Santa quietly peeked into the room through the half-closed door and saw little Sarah on the bed. The room was full of what appeared to be her family; there was the grandmother and the girl's brother he had met earlier that day. A woman, whom he guessed was Sarah's mother, stood by the bed, gently pushing Sarah's thin hair off her forehead.

Another woman, who he discovered later was Sarah's aunt, sat in a chair near the bed with a weary, sad look on her face. They were talking quietly, and Santa could sense the warmth and closeness of the family, and their love and concern for Sarah.

Taking a deep breath, and forcing a smile on his face, Santa entered the room, bellowing a hearty, "Ho, ho, ho!"

"Santa!" shrieked little Sarah weakly, as she tried to escape her bed to run to him.

Santa rushed to her side and gave her a warm hug. A child the tender age of his own son - nine years old - gazed up at him with wonder and excitement. Her skin was pale and her short tresses bore tell-tale bald patches from the effects of chemotherapy. But all he saw when he looked at her was a pair of huge, blue eyes. His heart melted, and he had to force himself to choke back tears.

Though his eyes were riveted upon Sarah's face, he could hear the gasps and quiet sobbing of the women in the room. As he and Sarah began talking, the family crept quietly to the bedside one by one, squeezing Santa's shoulder or his hand gratefully and whispering, "Thank you" as they gazed sincerely at him with shining eyes.

Santa and Sarah talked and talked, and she told him excitedly all the toys she wanted for Christmas, assuring him she'd been a very good girl that year. As their time together dwindled, Santa felt led in his spirit to pray for Sarah, and asked for permission from the girl's mother. She nodded in agreement and the entire family circled around Sarah's bed, holding hands.

Santa looked intensely at Sarah and asked her if she believed in angels, "Oh, yes, Santa... I do!" she exclaimed. "Well, I'm going to ask that angels watch over you," he said.

Laying one hand on the child's head, Santa closed his eyes and prayed. He asked that God touch little Sarah, and heal her body from this disease. He asked that angels minister to her, watch and keep her. And when he finished praying, still with eyes closed, he started singing, softly, "Silent Night, Holy Night... all is calm, all is bright..."

The family joined in, still holding hands, smiling at Sarah and crying tears of hope and joy for this moment, as Sarah beamed at them all. When the song ended, Santa sat on the side of the bed again and held Sarah's frail, small hands in his own.

"Now, Sarah," he said authoritatively, "you have a job to do, and that is to concentrate on getting well. I want you to have fun playing with your friends this summer and I expect to see you at my house at Mayfair Mall this time next year! "He knew it was risky proclaiming that to this little girl who had terminal cancer, but he 'had' to. He had to give her the greatest gift he could - not dolls or games or toys - but the gift of HOPE.

"Yes, Santa!" Sarah exclaimed, her eyes bright. He leaned down and kissed her on the forehead and left the room.

Out in the hall, the minute Santa's eyes met Rick's, a look passed between them and they wept unashamed. Sarah's mother and grandmother slipped out of the room quickly and rushed to Santa's side to thank him.

"My only child is the same age as Sarah" he explained quietly. "This is the least I could do." They nodded with understanding and hugged him.

One year later, Santa Mark was again back on the set in Milwaukee for his six-week, seasonal job that he so loved to do. Several weeks went by and then one day, a child came up to sit on his lap.

"Hi, Santa! Remember me?!"

"Of course I do!" Santa proclaimed (as he always does), smiling down at her. After all, the secret to being a 'good' Santa is to always make each child feel as if they are the 'only' child in the world at that moment.

"You came to see me in the hospital last year!" She said. Santa's jaw dropped. Tears immediately welled up in his eyes, and he grabbed this little miracle and held her to his chest.

"Sarah!" he exclaimed. He scarcely recognised her, for her hair was long and silky and her cheeks were rosy - so different from the little girl he had visited just a year before. He looked over and saw Sarah's mother and grandmother in the side-lines smiling and waving and wiping their eyes.

That was the best Christmas ever for Santa Claus.

He had witnessed – and been blessed to be instrumental in bringing about - this miracle of hope. This precious little child was healed. Cancer-free. Alive and well. He silently looked up to Heaven and humbly whispered, "Thank you, Father. 'Tis a very, Merry Christmas!"

By Susan Morton Leonard, Santa's wife.
Santa's name: Mark Leonard or Santa Mark

IF I HAD MY CHILD TO RAISE OVER AGAIN

If I had my child to raise over again,
I'd finger paint more, and point the finger less.
I'd do less correcting, and more connecting
I'd take my eyes off my watch, and watch with my eyes.
I would care to know less, and know to care more.
I'd take more hikes and fly more kites.
I'd stop playing serious, and seriously play.
I'd run through more fields, and gaze at more stars.
I'd do more hugging, and less tugging.
I would be firm less often, and affirm much more.
I'd build self-esteem first, and the house later.
I'd teach less about the love of power,
And more about the power of love.
It matters not whether my child is big or small.
From this day forth, I'll cherish it all.

By Diana Loomans.

AN ELF'S TALE

It was six o'clock at the mall, and I was as exhausted as an elf on Christmas Eve. In fact, I was an elf and it was Christmas Eve! That December of my sixteenth year, I'd been working two jobs to help my parents with my school tuition and to make a little extra holiday money. My second job was as an elf for Santa to help with kids' photos. Between my two jobs, I'd worked twelve hours straight the day before; on Christmas Eve, things were so busy at Santa land that I hadn't even had a coffee break all day. But this was it - only minutes more, and I'd have survived!

I looked over at Shelly, our manager, and she gave me an encouraging smile. She was the reason I'd made it through. She'd been thrown in as manager halfway through the season, and she'd made all the difference in the world. My job had changed from stress-filled to challenging. Instead of yelling at her workers to keep us in line, she encouraged us and stood behind us. She made us pull together as a team. Especially when things were at their craziest, she always had a smile and an encouraging word. Under her leadership, we'd achieved the highest number of mall photo sales in California.

I knew it was a difficult holiday season for her - she'd recently suffered a miscarriage. I hoped she knew how great she was and what a difference she'd made to all her workers, and to all the little children who'd come to have their pictures taken.

Our booth was open until seven; at six, things started to slow down and I finally took a break. Although I didn't have much money, I really wanted to buy a little gift for Shelly so that she'd know we appreciated her. I got to a store that sold soap and lotion just as they put the grate down. "Sorry, we're closed!" barked the clerk, who looked as tired as I was and didn't sound sorry at all.

I looked around and, to my dismay, found that all the stores had closed. I'd been so tired I hadn't noticed.

I was really bummed. I had been working all day and had missed buying her a present by one minute.

On my way back to the Santa booth, I saw that the department store Nordstrom was still open. Fearful that they too, would close at any moment, I hurried inside and followed the signs toward the Gift Gallery. As I rushed through the store, I began to feel very conspicuous. It seemed the other shoppers were all very well-dressed and wealthy - and here I was, a broke teenager in an elf costume. How could I even think I'd find something in such a posh store for under fifteen dollars?

I self-consciously jingled my way into the Gift Gallery. A woman sales associate, who also looked as if she'd just stepped off a fashion runway, came over and asked if she could help me. As she did, everyone in the department turned and stared.

As quietly as possible, I said, "No, that's okay. Just help somebody else."

She looked right at me and smiled. "No," she said. "I want to help you."

I told the woman who I was buying for and why, then I sheepishly admitted I only had fifteen dollars to spend. She looked as pleased and thoughtful as if I'd just asked to spend $1,500. By now, the department had emptied, but she carefully went around, selecting a few things that would make a nice basket. The total came to $14.09.

The store was closing; as she rang up the purchase, the lights were turned off.

I was thinking that if I could take them home and wrap them, I could make them really pretty but I didn't have time.

As if reading my mind, the saleslady asked, "Do you need this wrapped?"

"Yes," I said.

By now the store was closed. Over the intercom, a voice asked if there were still customers in the store. I knew this woman was probably as eager to get home on Christmas Eve as everybody else, and here she was stuck waiting on some kid with a measly purchase.

But she was gone in the back room a long time. When she returned, she brought out the most beautiful basket I'd ever seen. It was all wrapped up in silver and gold, and looked as if I'd spent fifty dollars on it - at least! I couldn't believe it. I was so happy!

When I thanked her, she said, "You elves are out in the mall spreading joy to so many people, I just wanted to bring a little joy to you."

"Merry Christmas, Shelly," I said, back at the booth. My manager gasped when she saw the present; she was so touched and happy that she started crying. I hoped it gave a happy start to her Christmas.

All through the holidays, I couldn't stop thinking about the kindness and effort of the saleswoman, and how much joy she had brought to me, and in turn to my manager. I thought the least I could do was to write a letter to the store and let them know about it. About a week later, I got a reply from the store, thanking me for writing.

I thought that was the end of it, until mid-January.

That's when I got a call from the sales associate, whose name was Stephanie. She wanted to take me to lunch. Me, a fifteen-dollar, sixteen-year-old customer!

When we met, Stephanie gave me a hug and a present, and told me this story.

She had walked into a recent employee meeting to find herself on the list of nominees to be named the Nordstrom All-Star. She was confused but excited, as she had never before been nominated. At the point in the meeting when the winner was announced, they called out her name - she'd won! When she went up to accept the award, her manager read my letter out loud. Everyone gave her a huge round of applause.

Winning meant that her picture was put up in the store lobby, she got new business cards with Nordstrom All-Star written on them, a 14-karat gold pin, a 100-dollar award, and was invited to represent her department at the regional meeting.

At the regional meeting, they read my letter and everyone gave Stephanie a standing ovation. "This is what we want all of our employees to be like!" said the manager who had read the letter. She got to meet three of the Nordstrom brothers, who were each very complimentary.

I was already a little overwhelmed when Stephanie took my hand. "But that's not the best part, Tyree," she said. "The day of that first store meeting, I took a list of the nominees, and put your letter behind it, with the 100-dollar bill behind that. I took it home and gave it to my father. He read everything and looked at me and said, "When do you find out who won?"

"I said, 'I won, Dad.'"

"He looked me right in the eye and said, 'Stephanie, I'm really proud of you.'"

Quietly, she said, "My dad has never said he was proud of me."

I think I'll remember that moment all my life. That was when I realised what a powerful gift appreciation can be. Shelly's appreciation of her workers had set into motion a chain of events - Stephanie's beautiful basket, my letter, Nordstrom's award - that had changed at least three lives.

Though I'd heard it all my life, it was the Christmas when I was an elf - and a broke teenager - that I truly came to understand that the littlest things can make the biggest difference.

By Tyree Dillingham – adapted from various versions on the internet.

WHAT HE VALUED MOST

It had been some time since Jack had seen the old man. College, girls, career, and life itself got in the way. In fact, Jack moved clear across the country in pursuit of his dreams. There, in the rush of his busy life, Jack had little time to think about the past and often no time to spend with his wife and son. He was working on his future, and nothing would stop him.

Over the phone, his mother told him, "Mr. Belser died last night. The funeral is Wednesday." Memories flashed through his mind like an old newsreel as he sat quietly remembering his childhood days.

"Jack, did you hear me?"

"Oh, sorry, Mom. Yes, I heard you. It's been so long since I thought of him. I'm sorry, but I honestly thought he died years ago," Jack said.

"Well, he didn't forget you. Every time I saw him he'd ask how you were doing. He'd reminisce about the many days you spent over 'his side of the fence' as he put it," Mom told him.

"I loved that old house he lived in," Jack said.

"You know, Jack, after your father died, Mr. Belser stepped in to make sure you had a man's influence in your life," she said.

"He's the one who taught me carpentry," he said. "I wouldn't be in this business if it weren't for him. He spent a lot of time teaching me things he thought were important... Mom, I'll be there for the funeral."

As busy as he was, he kept his word. Jack caught the next flight to his hometown. Mr. Belser's funeral was small and uneventful. He had no children of his own and most of his relatives had passed away. The night before he had to return home, Jack and his Mom stopped by to see the old house next door, one last time.

Standing in the doorway, Jack paused for a moment. It was like crossing over into another dimension, a leap through space and time. The house was exactly as he remembered. Every step held memories. Every picture, every piece of furniture...Jack stopped suddenly.

"What's wrong, Jack?" his Mom asked.

"The box is gone," he said.

"What box? " Mom asked.

"There was a small gold box that he kept locked on top of his desk. I must have asked him a thousand times what was inside. All he'd ever tell me was 'the thing I value most,'" Jack said.

It was gone. Everything about the house was exactly how Jack remembered it, except for the box. He figured someone from the Belser family had taken it.

 "Now I'll never know what was so valuable to him," Jack said. "I better get some sleep. I have an early flight home, Mom."

It had been about two weeks since Mr. Belser died. Returning home from work one day, Jack discovered a note in his mailbox. "Signature required on a package. No one at home. Please stop by the main post office within the next three days," the note read. Early the next day, Jack retrieved the package. The small box was old and looked like it had been mailed a hundred years ago. The handwriting was difficult to read, but the return address caught his attention.

'Mr Harold Belser', it read.

Jack took the box out to his car and ripped open the package. There inside was the gold box and an envelope. Jack's hands shook as he read the note inside.

"Upon my death, please forward this box and its contents to Jack Bennett. It's the thing I valued most in my life." A small key was taped to the letter. His heart racing, and as tears filled his eyes, Jack carefully unlocked the box. There inside he found a beautiful gold pocket watch. Running his fingers slowly over the finely etched casing, he unlatched the cover.

Inside he found these words engraved: "Jack, thanks for your time! Harold Belser."

"The thing he valued most...was...my time."

Jack held the watch for a few minutes, then called his office and cleared his appointments for the next two days. "Why?" Janet, his assistant, asked.

"I need some time to spend with my son," he said. "Oh, by the way, Janet...thanks for your time!"

Adapted from various versions on the internet

THE SEVEN WONDERS OF THE WORLD

Junior high school students in Chicago were studying the Seven Wonders of the World. At the end of the lesson, the students were asked to list what they considered to be the Seven Wonders of the World. Though there was some disagreement, the following received the most votes:

1. Egypt's Great Pyramids
2. The Taj Mahal in India
3. The Grand Canyon in Arizona
4. The Panama Canal
5. The Empire State Building
6. St. Peter's Basilica
7. China's Great Wall

While gathering the votes, the teacher noted that one student, a quiet girl, hadn't turned in her paper yet. So, she asked the girl if she was having trouble with her list. The quiet girl replied, "Yes, a little. I couldn't quite make up my mind because there were so many." The teacher said, "Well, tell us what you have, and maybe we can help."

The girl hesitated, then read, "I think the Seven Wonders of the World are:

1. To touch...
2. To taste...
3. To see...
4. To hear... (She hesitated a little, and then added...)
5. To feel...
6. To laugh...
7. And to love.

The room was so quiet; you could have heard a pin drop.

May this story serve as a gentle reminder to all of us that the things we overlook as simple and ordinary are often the most wonderful - and we don't have to travel anywhere special to experience them.

By Joy Garrison Wasson

TELL THEM NOW AND TELL THEM OFTEN!

I appreciate you for purchasing and reading my book. I am sincerely honoured to be a small part of your life! It felt nice to hear that, didn't it?

(By the way, I'm not just saying it to make a point, I sincerely mean it.)

Now think back to the last time YOU told someone that you appreciated them.

Can you remember how long ago it was?

Recently, I've been wondering why people tend to leave things unsaid. I'm talking about the important things like:

I appreciate you.

I'm proud of you.

I respect and admire you.

I'm glad you're my friend.

I'm sorry.

And, of course:

I love you!

I think we tend to neglect saying these things because we believe there will always be enough time. Most times we're right, but what if we're wrong and there is no time to say what we want to say? Eternity is a long time to leave something unsaid!

This week, I urge you to tell others how you feel. Tell them now and tell them often!

And don't just tell them because you may not have a chance later. Tell them because of how good it makes each and every one of us feel to hear these special phrases!

By the author

CHAPTER THREE :
ATTITUDE

A SIMPLE CUP OF TEA

There was a Japanese Zen master named Nan-in who lived during the Meiji era (1868-1912). During his days as a teacher, he was visited by a university professor curious about Zen.

Being polite, Nan-in served the professor a cup of tea.

As he poured, the professor's porcelain cup became full, but Nan-in kept on pouring. As the professor watched the cup overflow, he could no longer contain himself and said, "The cup is overfull. No more tea will go in!"

Nan-in turned to the professor and said, "Like the cup, your mind is too full of your own opinions and thoughts. How can I show you Zen unless you first empty your cup?"

A Zen Koan (a paradoxical statement or question used as a meditation) .

IT COULDN'T BE DONE

Somebody said that it couldn't be done
    But he, with a chuckle, replied
That "maybe it couldn't," but he would be one
    Who wouldn't say so till he'd tried?
So, he buckled right in with the trace of a grin
    On his face. If he worried he hid it.
He started to sing as he tackled the thing
    That couldn't be done, and he did it!

Somebody scoffed, "Oh, you'll never do that;
    At least no one ever has done it."
But he took off his coat and he took off his hat
    And the first thing we knew he'd begun it.
With a lift of his chin and a bit of a grin,
    Without any doubting or quiddit,
He started to sing as he tackled the thing
    That couldn't be done, and he did it.

There are thousands to tell you it cannot be done,
    There are thousands to prophesy failure,
There are thousands to point out to you one by one,
    The dangers that wait to assail you.
But just buckle in with a bit of a grin,
    Just take off your coat and go to it
Just start in to sing as you tackle the thing
    That "cannot be done," and you'll do it.

By Edgar Albert Guest

DO IT ANYWAY

The verses below reportedly were written on the wall of Mother Teresa's home for children in Calcutta, India, and are widely attributed to her. In any case, their association with Mother Teresa and the Missionaries of Charity has made them popular worldwide, expressing as they do, the spirit in which they lived their lives.

People are often unreasonable, irrational, and self-centred;
Forgive them anyway.

If you are kind, people may accuse you of selfish, ulterior motives;
Be kind anyway.

If you are successful, you will win some unfaithful friends and some genuine enemies;
Succeed anyway.

If you are honest and sincere people may deceive you;
Be honest and sincere anyway.

What you spend years creating, others could destroy overnight;
Create anyway.

If you find serenity and happiness, some may be jealous;
Be happy anyway.

The good you do today will often be forgotten;
Do good anyway.

Give the best you have, and it will never be enough;
Give your best anyway.

In the final analysis, it is between you and God;
It was never between you and them anyway.

Mother Teresa
Adapted from various versions on the internet

———— ▪ ▪ ▪ ————

ATTITUDE IS EVERYTHING

Jerry was the kind of guy you love to hate. He was always in a good mood and always had something positive to say. When someone would ask him how he was doing, he would reply, "If I were any better, I would be twins!"

He was a unique manager because he had several waiters who had followed him around from restaurant to restaurant. The reason the waiters followed Jerry was because of his attitude. He was a natural motivator. If an employee was having a bad day, Jerry was there telling the employee how to look on the positive side of the situation.

Seeing this style really made me curious, so one day I went up to Jerry and asked him, "I don't get it! You can't be a positive person all of the time. How do you do it?"

Jerry replied, "Each morning I wake up and say to myself, 'Jerry, you have two choices today. You can choose to be in a good mood or you can choose to be in a bad mood.' I choose to be in a good mood. Each time something bad happens, I can choose to be a victim or I can choose to learn from it. I choose to learn from it. Every time someone comes to me complaining, I can choose to accept their complaining or I can point out the positive side of life. I choose the positive side of life."

"Yeah, right, it's not that easy," I protested.

"Yes it is," Jerry said. "Life is all about choices. When you cut away all the junk, every situation is a choice. You choose how you react to situations. You choose how people will affect your mood. You choose to be in a good mood or bad mood. The bottom line: It's your choice how you live life."

I reflected on what Jerry said. Soon thereafter, I left the restaurant industry to start my own business. We lost touch, but I often thought about him when I made a choice about life instead of reacting to it.

Several years later, I heard that Jerry did something you are never supposed to do in a restaurant business: he left the back door open one morning, and was held up at gunpoint by three armed robbers. While trying to open the safe, his hand, shaking from nervousness, slipped off the combination. The robbers panicked and shot him. Luckily, Jerry was found relatively quickly and rushed to the local trauma centre.

After 18 hours of surgery and weeks of intensive care, Jerry was released from the hospital with fragments of the bullets still in his body. I saw Jerry about six months after the accident. When I asked him how he was, he replied, "If I were any better, I'd be twins. Want to see my scars?"

47

I declined to see his wounds, but did ask him what had gone through his mind as the robbery took place. "The first thing that went through my mind was that I should have locked the back door," Jerry replied. "Then, as I lay on the floor, I remembered that I had two choices: I could choose to live, or I could choose to die. I chose to live."

"Weren't you scared? Did you lose consciousness?" I asked.

Jerry continued, "The paramedics were great. They kept telling me I was going to be fine. But when they wheeled me into the emergency room and I saw the expressions on the faces of the doctors and nurses, I got really scared. In their eyes, I read, 'He's a dead man'. I knew I needed to take action."

"What did you do?" I asked.

"Well, there was a big, burly nurse shouting questions at me," said Jerry. 'She asked if I was allergic to anything. 'Yes,' I replied. The doctors and nurses stopped working as they waited for my reply... I took a deep breath and yelled, 'Bullets!' Over their laughter, I told them, 'I am choosing to live. Operate on me as if I am alive, not dead.'"

Jerry lived, thanks to the skill of his doctors, but also because of his amazing attitude. I learned from him that every day we have the choice to live fully. Attitude, after all, is everything.

By Francie Baltazar-Schwartz

THE ARROGANT NEW MANAGING DIRECTOR

A company hired a new Managing Director. This new boss was determined to rid the company of all slackers.

While taking a tour around the facilities, the MD noticed a guy leaning on a wall. The room was full of workers and he thought this was his chance to show everyone he meant business!

The MD walked up to the man and asked, "And how much money do you make?"

A bit surprised, the young man looked at him and replied, "I make £500 a week, why do you ask?"

The MD took out some cash and handed the man £500 and then screamed to him, "Here! This is your last pay; now get out, because you are fired!"

That was his first firing and he felt pretty good about it! He looked around triumphantly and asked the workers, "Does anybody know what that slacker did here?"

With a large grin, one of the workers muttered, "He's the pizza delivery man, sir!"

Great Attitude, Great Results, Bad Attitude.....

Author Unknown

THE TROUBLE TREE

The carpenter I hired to help me restore an old farmhouse had just finished a rough first day on the job. A flat tire made him lose an hour of work, his electric saw quit, and now his ancient pickup truck refused to start. While I drove him home, he sat in stony silence.

On arriving, he invited me in to meet his family. As we walked toward the front door, he paused briefly at a small tree, touching the tips of the branches with both hands. When opening the door he underwent an amazing transformation. His tanned face was wreathed in smiles and he hugged his two small children and gave his wife a kiss.

Afterwards, he walked me to the car. We passed the tree and my curiosity got the better of me. I asked him about what I had seen him do earlier.

"Oh, that's my trouble tree," he replied. "I know I can't help having troubles on the job, but one thing's for sure; troubles don't belong in the house with my wife and the children. So, I just hang them on the tree every night when I come home. Then in the morning I pick them up again."

He paused. "Funny thing is," he smiled, "when I come out in the morning to pick them up, there aren't nearly as many as I remember hanging up the night before!"

Author Unknown

■ ■ ■

CHAPTER FOUR : BELIEF

THE CORPSE

A psychiatrist was treating a man who believed he was a corpse. Despite all the psychiatrist's logical arguments, the man persisted in his belief. In a flash of inspiration, the psychiatrist asked the man, "Do corpses bleed?" The patient replied, "That's ridiculous, of course corpses don't bleed." After first asking permission, the psychiatrist pricked the man's finger and produced a drop of bright red blood. The patient looked at his bleeding finger with abject astonishment and exclaimed: "I'll be damned, corpses do bleed!"

Abraham Maslow

HAVE YOU SWALLOWED ANY SNAKES RECENTLY?

A foolish peasant was sent to visit his master's house. The master brought him into the study and offered him some soup, but just as the peasant was about to drink it, he noticed a small snake in his bowl. Not wanting to offend his master he drank it anyway, and within a few days fell so ill that he was brought back to the house.

51

The master again took him into his study and prepared some medicine in a small bowl which he then gave to the peasant. Just as the peasant was about to drink the medicine, he noticed another snake in the bowl. This time he pointed it out and loudly complained that this was the reason he was sick in the first place.

Roaring with laughter, the master pointed to the ceiling where a large bow was hanging. "It is the reflection of the bow you are seeing," he said. "There is no snake at all."

The peasant looked again and, sure enough, there was no snake in his bowl, only a reflection. He left the house without taking the medicine and regained his health within the day.

Zen Parable

When we accept limitations about ourselves and our world, we have swallowed imaginary mental snakes. And they are always real until we start to think otherwise. Once your subconscious mind has accepted a belief or idea, whether true or not, it will continually feed your thoughts to support that belief.

Our mind will distort our perception of reality to make it conform to our beliefs. Think you are worthless? Or that it's hard to achieve things? Believe you are susceptible to poor health? Your mind will find irrefutable evidence to support those beliefs and will work overtime to manifest those realities.

On the other hand, if you believe that you are a loving, kind person, and that you deserve to make your dreams come true - and you believe in your own vibrant health - you'll find yourself surrounded by equally strong evidence supporting those beliefs.

Choose your beliefs wisely!

IF YOU THINK YOU CAN

This following story has been used as a motivational lesson that demonstrates the power of positive thinking and belief. The basic story has persisted in the form of an urban legend and as an introductory scene in the film 'Good Will Hunting' (1997).

The origin of this famous story is an event in George Bernard Dantzig's life, while he was a graduate student at the University of California, Berkeley in 1939.

Near the beginning of a class for which Dantzig was late, two examples of famously unsolved statistics problems were on the blackboard. When Dantzig arrived, he assumed that the two problems were a homework assignment and wrote them down. According to Dantzig, the problems "seemed to be a little harder than usual", but a few days later he handed in completed solutions for the two problems, still believing that they were an assignment that was overdue.

Six weeks later, Dantzig received a visit from an excited Professor Neyman, who was eager to tell him that the homework problems he had solved were two of the most famous unsolved problems in statistics, mind teasers that even Einstein hadn't been able to solve.

Adapted from various versions on the internet

THE CANCER SURVIVORS' STUDY

A woman had interviewed 100 "cancer survivors" in hopes of finding out what these survivors had in common. She described a cancer survivor as someone who had been given a terminal diagnosis of cancer with a poor prognosis for recovery, but who was still alive and healthy, enjoying life ten or twelve years later. Interestingly enough, she could find no common patterns in the treatment received by these people. Different people received different treatments, including chemotherapy, radiation therapy, nutrition programs, surgery, spiritual healing and so on. However, there was one thing that all these survivors shared: they all believed that the method of treatment they were getting was going to work for them. The belief, not the treatment, made the difference.

From the book 'Beliefs' by Robert Dilts,
Tim Hallbom and Suzi Smith.

YOU'LL SEE IT WHEN YOU BELIEVE IT

There was a business executive who was deep in debt and could see no way out.

Creditors were closing in on him. Suppliers were demanding payment. He sat on the park bench, head in hands, wondering if anything could save his company from bankruptcy.

Suddenly an old man appeared before him. "I can see that something is troubling you," he said.

After listening to the executive's woes, the old man said, "I believe I can help you."

He asked the man his name, wrote out a cheque and pushed it into his hand saying, "Take this money. Meet me here exactly one year from today, and you can pay me back at that time."

Then he turned and disappeared as quickly as he had come.

The business executive saw in his hand a cheque for $500,000, signed by John D. Rockefeller, then one of the richest men in the world!

"I can erase my money worries in an instant!" he realised. But instead, the executive decided to put the uncashed cheque in his safe. Just knowing it was there might give him the strength to work out a way to save his business, he thought.

With renewed optimism, he negotiated better deals and extended terms of payment. He closed several big sales. Within a few months, he was out of debt and making money once again.

Exactly one year later, he returned to the park with the uncashed cheque. At the agreed-upon time, the old man appeared. But just as the executive was about to hand back the cheque and share his success story, a nurse came running up and grabbed the old man.

"I'm so glad I caught him!" she cried. "I hope he hasn't been bothering you. He's always escaping from the rest home and telling people he's John D. Rockefeller."

And she led the old man away by the arm.

The astonished executive just stood there, stunned. All year long he'd been wheeling and dealing, buying and selling, convinced he had half a million dollars behind him.

Suddenly, he realised that it wasn't the money, real or imagined, that had turned his life around. It was his newfound belief that gave him the power to achieve anything he went after.

Author Unknown

I BELIEVE

I believe-

That we don't have to change friends if we understand that friends change.

I believe-

That no matter how good a friend is, they're going to hurt you every once in a while and you must forgive them for that.

I believe-

That true friendship continues to grow, even over the longest distance.
The same goes for true love.

I believe-

That you can do something in an instant that will give you heartache for life.

I believe-

That it's taking me a long time to become the person I want to be.

I believe-

That you should always leave loved ones with loving words. It may be the last time you see them.

I believe-

That you can keep going long after you can't.

I believe-

That we are responsible for what we do, no matter how we feel.

I believe-

That either you control your attitude or it controls you.

I believe-

That regardless of how hot and steamy a relationship is at first, the passion fades and there had better be something else to take its place.

I believe-

That heroes are the people who do what has to be done when it needs to be done, regardless of the consequences.

I believe-

That money is a lousy way of keeping score.

I believe-

That my best friend and I can do anything or nothing and have the best time!

I believe-

That sometimes the people you expect to kick you when you're down, will be the ones to help you get back up.

I believe-

That sometimes when I'm angry I have the right to be angry, but that doesn't give me the right to be cruel.

I believe-

That just because someone doesn't love you the way you want them to doesn't mean they don't love you with all they have.

I believe-

That maturity has more to do with the types of experiences you've had and what you've learned from them and less to do with how many birthdays you've celebrated.

I believe-

That it isn't always enough to be forgiven by others. Sometimes you have to learn to forgive yourself.

I believe-

That no matter how bad your heart is broken, the world doesn't stop for your grief.

I believe-

That our background and circumstances may have influenced who we are, but we are responsible for who we become.

I believe-

That just because two people argue, it doesn't mean they

don't love each other, and just because they don't argue, it doesn't mean they do.

I believe-

That you shouldn't be so eager to find out a secret. It could change your life forever.

I believe-

That two people can look at the exact same thing and see something totally different.

I believe-

That your life can be changed in a matter of hours by people who don't even know you.

I believe-

That even when you think you have no more to give, when a friend cries out to you - you will find the strength to help.

I believe-

That credentials on the wall do not make you a decent human being.

I believe-

That the people you care about most in life are the essence of life.

Tell them today how much you love them and what they mean to you.

Adapted from various versions on the internet

CLASS "A" CHILDREN

Many years ago, an experiment in education was carried out in secrecy at a school in England. The school had two classes for the same age of children. At the end of the school year an examination was held, in order to select the children for the classes of next year. However, the results of the exam were never revealed. In secrecy, with only the headmaster and the psychologists involved in the experiment knowing the truth, the child who came first in the exam was placed in the same class with the children who came fourth and fifth, eighth and ninth, twelfth and thirteenth, and so on. The children who came second and third in the exam were placed in the other class, with the children who came sixth and seventh, tenth and eleventh, and so on.

In other words, based on their performance in the exam, the higher-performing and lower - performing children were split evenly between the two classes. Teachers for the next year were carefully selected for equal ability and experience. Even the classrooms were chosen with similar facilities. Everything was made as equal as possible, except for one thing; one was called Class "A" and the other, Class "B". Whereas, in fact, the classes had children of equal ability, in everyone's minds the children in Class A were the clever ones and the kids of Class B were not so clever. Some of the parents of the Class A children were pleasantly surprised that their child had done so well and rewarded them with presents and praise, whereas the parents of some of the Class B kids berated their children for not working hard enough and took away some of their privileges. Even the teachers taught the Class B kids in a different manner, not expecting much from them. For a whole year the illusion was maintained. Then there was another end-of-year exam.

The results were chilling, but not surprising. The children of Class A performed so much better than those of Class B. In fact, the results were just as if they had been the top half chosen from last year's exam. They had become Class "A" children. And those in the other group, though equal the year before, had now become Class "B" kids. That was what they were told for a whole year, that was how they were treated, and that was what they believed - so that was what they became.

Author Unknown

CHAPTER FIVE : CHANGE

DESTROYING AND REBUILDING

I am invited to go to "the site of a Zen Buddhist temple". When I get there, I am surprised to see that the extraordinarily beautiful building, which is situated in the middle of a vast forest, is right next to a huge piece of waste ground.

I ask what the waste ground is for and the man in charge explains (I can't verify if it is true, but it must be):

"That is where we will build the next temple.

"Every twenty years, we destroy the temple you see before you now and rebuild it again on the site next to it.

"This means that the monks who have trained as carpenters, stonemasons and architects are always using their practical skills and passing them on to their apprentices.

"It also shows them that nothing in this life is eternal and that even temples are in need of constant improvement."

November 11, 2017 blog post by Paulo Coelho

THE EAGLE

The Eagle has the longest life span of any bird, living up to seventy years. But to reach this age the eagle must make a tough decision.

In its forties, its long and flexible talons can no longer grab the prey that serves as its food. Its long and sharp beak becomes bent and due to the thick feathers, its aged and heavy wings become stuck to its chest, making it difficult to fly.

It is then that the eagle is left with only two choices... to die or go through a painful process of change which lasts 150 days.

The process requires that the eagle fly up to a mountain top and sit on its nest. There, the eagle hits its beak against a rock until the beak is knocked off. The eagle will then wait for a new beak to grow back and then it will pluck out its talons. Once its new talons grow back, the eagle then starts plucking its old-aged feathers.

And after five months, the eagle takes its famous flight of rebirth and lives for around thirty more years.

Adapted from various versions on the internet

THE FIVE MONKEYS EXPERIMENT

In the 1980s an experiment on monkeys was conducted in a research study on social dynamics. The researcher put five monkeys in a large cage. High up at the top of the cage, well beyond the reach of the monkeys, was a bunch of bananas. Underneath the bananas was a ladder.

The monkeys immediately spotted the bananas and one began to climb the ladder. As he got to the top and reached for the bananas, the experimenter sprayed him with a stream of cold water. Then, he proceeded to spray each of the other monkeys.

The monkey on the ladder scrambled off. And all five sat for a time on the floor, wet, cold and bewildered. Soon, though, the temptation of the bananas was too great, and another monkey began to climb the ladder. Again, the experimenter sprayed the ambitious monkey with cold water and all the other monkeys as well. When a third monkey tried to climb the ladder, the other monkeys, wanting to avoid the cold spray, pulled him off the ladder and beat him.

A few days later, the researcher removed one of the five monkeys and a new monkey was introduced to the group. Spotting the bananas, the new monkey naively began to climb the ladder. The original four monkeys pulled him off and beat him.

Here's where it gets interesting. The experimenter removed a second original monkey from the cage and replaced him with a new monkey. Again, the new monkey began to climb the ladder and, again, the other monkeys pulled him off and beat him - including the monkey who had never been sprayed.

Gradually, all the monkeys were replaced with new ones. The new monkeys continued with the same treatment of any monkey who attempted to reach the bananas. They would pull him off and beat him up, despite the fact that none of them experienced the cold-water treatment. They had all learned that they should never go for the bananas.

This experiment describes perfectly how our society often reacts when someone attempts to change things.

Adapted from various versions on the internet

THERE'S A HOLE IN MY SIDEWALK

Chapter One
    I walk down the street.
There is a deep hole in the sidewalk.
I fall in.
I am lost …. I am helpless.
It isn't my fault.
It takes forever to find a way out.

Chapter Two
    I walk down the street.
There is a deep hole in the sidewalk.
I pretend that I don't see it.
I fall in again.
I can't believe I am in this same place.
But, it isn't my fault.
It still takes a long time to get out.

65

Chapter Three

I walk down the same street.
There is a deep hole in the sidewalk.
I see it is there.
I still fall in ... it's a habit ... but, my eyes are open.
I know where I am.
It is my fault.
I get out immediately.

Chapter Four

I walk down the same street.
There is a deep hole in the sidewalk.
I walk around it.

Chapter Five

I walk down another street.

These steps, in summary, are:

• Become aware of the hole or pattern in your life that you wish to change.

• Start to consciously notice the times when you "fall in."

• Start to notice that you are about to "fall in" before you do.

• Start to avoid the same situations and paths that have led you to "falling in".

• Start to choose an entirely different route!

'The Romance of Self-Discovery', an autobiography in five short chapters by Portia Nelson

THE IMPORTANCE OF
THE CAT IN MEDITATION

A great Zen master, in charge of the monastery of Mayu Kagi, owned a cat, who was the real love of his life. During meditation classes, he always kept the cat by his side in order to enjoy its company as much as possible.

One morning, the master, who was already quite old, was found dead. The oldest disciple took his place.

'What shall we do with the cat?' asked the other monks.

In homage to the memory of his former teacher, the new master decided to allow the cat to continue attending the classes on Zen Buddhism.

Some disciples from neighbouring monasteries, who travelled widely in the region, discovered that, in one of the most famous temples in the area, a cat took part in the meditations. The story began to spread.

Many years passed. The cat died, but the students at the monastery were so used to its presence that they acquired another cat. Meanwhile, the other temples began introducing cats into their meditation classes; they believed that the cat was the one actually responsible for Mayu Kagi's fame and for the quality of his teaching, forgetting what an excellent teacher the former master had been.

A generation passed, and technical treatises on the importance of the cat in Zen meditation began to be published. A university professor developed a thesis, accepted by the academic community, that the cat had the ability to increase human concentration and to eliminate negative energy.

67

And thus, for a century, the cat was considered to be an essential part of the study of Zen Buddhism in that region.

Then a master arrived who was allergic to cat hair. He decided to remove the cat from his daily practices with the students.

Everyone protested, but the master insisted. Since he was a gifted teacher, the students continued to make progress, despite the cat's absence.

Gradually, monasteries – always in search of new ideas and weary of having to feed so many cats – began to remove cats from the classroom. Over the next twenty years, revolutionary new theses were written, bearing persuasive titles like 'The Importance of Meditating Without a Cat' or 'Balancing the Zen Universe by the Power of One's Mind Alone and Without the Aid of Animals'.

Another century passed, and the cat vanished completely from the Zen meditation ritual in that region. But it took two hundred years for everything to return to normal - all because, during that time, no one thought to ask why the cat was there.

A writer, who learned of this story centuries later, wrote in his diary, "and how many of us, in our own lives, ever dare to ask: why do I behave in such and such a way? In what we do, how far are we too using futile 'cats' that we do not have the courage to get rid of because we were told that the 'cats' were important in keeping everything running smoothly?"

August 13, 2007 blog post by Paulo Coelho

OUR DEEPEST FEAR

Our deepest fear is not that we are inadequate.
Our deepest fear is that we are powerful
beyond measure.
It is our light, not our darkness
That most frightens us.

We ask ourselves
Who am I to be brilliant, gorgeous, talented, fabulous?
Actually, who are you not to be?
You are a child of God.

Your playing small
Does not serve the world.
There's nothing enlightened about shrinking
So that other people won't feel insecure around you.

We are all meant to shine,
As children do.
We were born to make manifest
The glory of God that is within us.

It's not just in some of us;
It's in everyone.
And as we let our own light shine,
We unconsciously give other people
    permission to do the same.

As we're liberated from our own fear,
Our presence automatically liberates others.

By Marianne Williamson

69

CHAPTER SIX : FAITH

THE BEST RELIGION

In a round table discussion about religion and freedom in which Dalai Lama and myself were participating at recess, I maliciously, and also with interest, asked him, "Your holiness, what is the best religion?"

I thought he would say, "The Tibetan Buddhism" or "The oriental religions, much older than Christianity."

The Dalai Lama paused, smiled and looked me in the eyes...which surprised me because I knew of the malice contained in my question.

He answered: "The best religion is the one that gets you closest to God. It is the one that makes you a better person."

To get out of my embarrassment with such a wise answer, I asked: "What is it that makes me better?"

He responded:

"Whatever makes you:
More compassionate,
More sensible,
More detached,
More loving,
More humanitarian,

More responsible,
More ethical.

The religion that will do that for you is the best religion."

I was silent for a moment, marvelling, and even today think of his wise and irrefutable response.

He continued, "I am not interested, my friend, about your religion or if you are religious or not. What really is important to me is your behaviour in front of your peers, family, work, community, and in front of the world.

"Remember, the universe is the echo of our actions and our thoughts.

"The law of action and reaction is not exclusively for physics. It is also of human relations.

"If I act with goodness, I will receive goodness. If I act with evil, I will get evil.

"What our grandparents told us is the pure truth. You will always have what you desire for others. Being happy is not a matter of destiny. It is a matter of options."

Finally, he said:

"Take care of your Thoughts because they will become Words.

Take care of your Words because they will become Actions.

Take care of your Actions because they will become Habits.

Take care of your Habits because they will form your Character.

Take care of your Character because it will form your Destiny.

And your Destiny will be your Life

And...

There is no religion higher than the Truth."

By Leonardo Boff, Brazilian theologian and renovator of the Theology of Freedom

THIS TOO SHALL PASS

There lived a king in a Middle Eastern land who was continuously torn between happiness and despondency. The slightest thing would cause him great upset or provoke an intense reaction and his happiness would quickly turn into disappointment and despair. A time came when the king finally got tired of himself and of his life so he began to seek a way out. He sent for a wise man that lived in the kingdom, who was reputed to be enlightened.

When the wise man arrived, the king said to him, "I want to be like you. Can you give me something that will bring balance, serenity and wisdom into my life? I will pay any price you ask."

The wise man said, "I may be able to help you but the price is so great that your entire kingdom would not be sufficient payment for it. Therefore, it will be a gift to you if you will honour it." The king gave his assurances and the wise man left. A few weeks later, he returned and handed the king an ornate box carved in jade. The king opened the box and found a simple gold ring inside. Some letters were inscribed on the ring. The inscription read: 'This, too, shall pass.'

"What is the meaning of this?" asked the king. The wise man replied, "Wear this ring always. Whatever happens, before you call it good or bad, touch this ring and read the inscription. That way, you will always be at peace."

Ancient Sufi story

THE PARABLE OF THE CHINESE FARMER

Once there was a Chinese farmer who worked his poor farm together with his son and their horse. When the horse ran off one day, neighbours came to say, "How unfortunate for you!" The farmer replied, "Maybe yes, maybe no."

When the horse returned, followed by a herd of wild horses, the neighbours gathered around and exclaimed, "What good luck for you!" The farmer stayed calm and replied, "Maybe yes, maybe no."

While trying to tame one of wild horses, the farmer's son fell, and broke his leg. He had to rest up and couldn't help with the farm chores. "How sad for you," the neighbours cried. "Maybe yes, maybe no," said the farmer.

Shortly thereafter, a neighbouring army threatened the farmer's village. All the young men in the village were drafted to fight the invaders. Many died. But the farmer's son had been left out of the fighting because of his broken leg. "What a good thing your son couldn't fight!" people said to the farmer, "Maybe yes, maybe no," replied the farmer.

Adapted from various versions on the internet

CHEYENNE

Watch out! You nearly broad-sided that car," my father yelled at me. "Can't you do anything right?"

Those words hurt worse than blows. I turned my head toward the elderly man in the seat beside me, daring me to challenge him. A lump rose in my throat as I averted my eyes. I wasn't prepared for another battle.

"I saw the car, Dad. Please don't yell at me when I'm driving."

My voice was measured and steady, sounding far calmer than I really felt.

Dad glared at me, then turned away and settled back. At home I left Dad in front of the television and went outside to collect my thoughts...dark, heavy clouds hung in the air with a promise of rain. The rumble of distant thunder seemed to echo my inner turmoil. What could I do about him?

Dad had been a lumberjack in Washington and Oregon. He had enjoyed being outdoors and had revelled in pitting his strength against the forces of nature. He had entered gruelling lumberjack competitions, and had placed often. The shelves in his house were filled with trophies that attested to his prowess.

The years marched on relentlessly. The first time he couldn't lift a heavy log, he joked about it; but later that same day I saw him outside alone, straining to lift it. He became irritable whenever anyone teased him about his advancing age, or when he couldn't do something he had done as a younger man.

Four days after his sixty-seventh birthday, he had a heart attack. An ambulance sped him to the hospital while a paramedic administered CPR to keep blood and oxygen flowing.

At the hospital, Dad was rushed into an operating room. He was lucky; he survived, but something inside Dad died. His zest for life was gone. He obstinately refused to follow doctor's orders. Suggestions and offers of help were turned aside with sarcasm and insults. The number of visitors thinned, and then finally stopped altogether. Dad was left alone.

My husband, Dick, and I asked Dad to come live with us on our small farm. We hoped the fresh air and rustic atmosphere would help him adjust.

Within a week of him moving in, I regretted the invitation. It seemed nothing was satisfactory. He criticised everything I did. I became frustrated and moody. Soon I was taking my pent-up anger out on Dick. We began to bicker and argue.

Alarmed, Dick sought out our pastor and explained the situation. The clergyman set up weekly counselling appointments for us. At the close of each session he prayed, asking God to soothe Dad's troubled mind.

But the months wore on and God was silent. Something had to be done and it was up to me to do it.

The next day I sat down with the phone book and methodically called each of the mental health clinics listed in the Yellow Pages. I explained my problem to each of the sympathetic voices that answered in vain. Just when I was giving up hope, one of the voices suddenly exclaimed,

"I just read something that might help you! Let me go get the article."

I listened as she read. The article described a remarkable study done at a nursing home. All of the patients were under treatment for chronic depression. Yet their attitudes had improved dramatically when they were given responsibility for a dog.

I drove to the animal shelter that afternoon. After I filled out a questionnaire, a uniformed officer led me to the kennels. The odour of disinfectant stung my nostrils as I moved down the row of pens. Each contained five to seven dogs; long-haired dogs, curly-haired dogs, black dogs, spotted dogs all jumping up, trying to reach me.

I studied each one but rejected one after the other for various reasons: too big, too small, too much hair. As I neared the last pen, a dog in the shadows of the far corner struggled to his feet, walked to the front of the run and sat down. It was a pointer, one of the dog world's aristocrats. But this dog was a caricature of the breed.

Years had etched his face and muzzle with shades of grey. His hip bones jutted out in lopsided triangles. But it was his eyes that caught and held my attention. Calm and clear, they beheld me unwaveringly.

I pointed to the dog. "Can you tell me about him?" The officer looked, then shook his head in puzzlement. "He's a funny one. Appeared out of nowhere and sat in front of the gate. We brought him in, figuring someone would be right down to claim him. That was two weeks ago and we've heard nothing. His time is up tomorrow," he gestured helplessly.

As the words sank in, I turned to the man in horror. "You mean you're going to kill him?"

"Ma'am," he said gently, "that's our policy. We don't have room for every unclaimed dog."

I looked at the pointer again. The calm brown eyes awaited my decision. "I'll take him," I said. I drove home with the dog on the front seat beside me. When I reached the house, I honked the horn twice. I was helping my prize out of the car when Dad shuffled onto the front porch. "Ta-da! Look what I got for you, Dad!" I said, excitedly.

Dad looked, and then wrinkled his face in disgust. "If I had wanted a dog I would have gotten one. And I would have picked out a better specimen than that bag of bones. Keep it! I don't want it!" Dad waved his arm scornfully and turned back toward the house.

Anger rose inside me. It squeezed together my throat muscles and pounded into my temples. "You'd better get used to him, Dad. He's staying!"

Dad ignored me. "Did you hear me, Dad?" I screamed. At those words Dad whirled angrily, his hands clenched at his sides, his eyes narrowed and blazing with hate. We stood glaring at each other like duellists, when suddenly the pointer pulled free from my grasp. He wobbled toward my dad and sat down in front of him. Then slowly, carefully, he raised his paw.

Dad's lower jaw trembled as he stared at the uplifted paw. Confusion replaced the anger in his eyes. The pointer waited patiently. Then suddenly Dad was on his knees hugging the animal.

It was the beginning of a warm and intimate friendship. Dad named the pointer Cheyenne. Together, he and Cheyenne explored the community. They spent long hours walking down dusty lanes. They spent reflective moments on the banks of streams, angling for tasty trout. They even started to attend Sunday services together, Dad sitting in a pew and Cheyenne lying quietly at his feet.

Dad and Cheyenne were inseparable throughout the next three years. Dad's bitterness faded, and he and Cheyenne made many friends. Then late one night I was startled to feel Cheyenne's cold nose burrowing through our bed covers. He had never before come into our bedroom at night. I woke Dick, put on my robe, and ran into my father's room. Dad lay in his bed, his face serene. But his spirit had left quietly sometime during the night.

Two days later my shock and grief deepened when I discovered Cheyenne lying dead beside Dad's bed. I wrapped his still form in the rag rug he had slept on. As Dick and I buried him near a favourite fishing hole, I silently thanked the dog for the help he had given me in restoring Dad's peace of mind.

The morning of Dad's funeral dawned, overcast and dreary. This day looks like the way I feel, I thought, as I walked down the aisle to the pews reserved for family. I was surprised to see the many friends Dad and Cheyenne had made, filling the church. The pastor began his eulogy. It was a tribute to both Dad and the dog who had changed his life.

And then the pastor turned to Hebrews 13:2. "Do not neglect to show hospitality to strangers, for by this some have entertained angels without knowing it."

"I've often thanked God for sending that angel," he said.

For me, the past dropped into place, completing a puzzle that I had not seen before; the sympathetic voice that had just read the right article. Cheyenne's unexpected appearance at the animal shelter...his calm acceptance and complete devotion to my father...and the proximity of their deaths. And suddenly I understood. I knew that God had answered my prayers after all.

Life is too short for drama or petty things, so laugh hard, love truly and forgive quickly. Live while you are alive. Forgive now those who made you cry. You might not get a second chance.

And remember...God answers our prayers in His time... not ours...

By Catherine Moore

RIGHT AND WRONG

When Bankei, a Japanese Master, held his seclusion-weeks of meditation, pupils from many parts of Japan came to attend. During one of these gatherings a pupil was caught stealing. The matter was reported to Bankei with the request that the culprit be expelled. Bankei ignored the case.

Later the pupil was caught in a similar act, and again Bankei disregarded the matter. This angered the other pupils, who drew up a petition asking for the dismissal of the thief, stating that otherwise they would leave as a body.

When Bankei had read the petition, he called everyone before him. "You are wise brothers," he told them. "You know what is right and what is not right. You may go somewhere else to study if you wish, but this poor brother does not even know right from wrong. Who will teach him if I do not? I am going to keep him here even if all the rest of you leave."

A torrent of tears cleansed the face of the brother who had stolen. All desire to steal had vanished.

A Zen Parable

IT WILL PASS

A student went to his meditation teacher and said, "My meditation is horrible! I feel so distracted, or my legs ache, or I'm constantly falling asleep. It's just horrible!"

"It will pass," the teacher said, matter-of-factly.

A week later, the student came back to his teacher. "My meditation is wonderful! I feel so aware, so peaceful, so alive! It's just wonderful!'

"It will pass," the teacher replied, matter-of-factly.

A Zen story

CHAPTER SEVEN : FORGIVENESS

CORRIE ten BOOM

To forgive is to set a prisoner free and to discover that the prisoner was you.

Corrie ten Boom

This quote hit me smack in the face and encouraged me to find out more about Corrie ten Bloom.

Her family had hidden Jews in their house in the Netherlands. The Gestapo found the family out, and sent Corrie and her family to Ravensbruck concentration camp. After the war, while at a church service in Munich, she came face-to-face with one of the former Ravensbruck prison guards. Corrie had just delivered a message of God's forgiveness and the former guard, not recognizing her, asked Corrie personally for forgiveness for the atrocities that he had committed. Corrie struggled within herself and found that she could not forgive him at first, but she quickly prayed and found the strength to accept his extended hand.

Adapted from various versions on the internet

LETTING GO

I have read this powerful Buddhist story many times. Every time I read this, it comes with a whole new meaning and leaves me with a sense of freedom as I am reminded of the power of flexibility, understanding and, more importantly...letting go.

A senior and a junior monk are traveling together. They come to a river with a very strong current. A pretty young woman is walking along the riverbank looking very upset. "What's the matter?" asks the senior monk. "I'm really worried ", replies the girl, "because my father is ill and I need to cross the river in order to get to him but the bridge has collapsed. Do you know where the next bridge is?"

"Oh, it's miles away," replies the monk. "But don't worry; I can carry you over the water." The girl gratefully accepts the offer of help and the senior monk carries her on his back to the other side of the river, puts her down and says goodbye.

As the monks continue on their way, the junior monk is very troubled by what has happened. He knows that monks are not allowed to touch women and he is furious that the senior monk has broken his vows. He continues to fume and agonise over this for some time. Finally, he can bear it no longer and he confronts the senior monk.

"Brother, our spiritual training teaches us to avoid any contact with women, but you picked that one up on your shoulders and carried her over the river!"

"Brother," the older monk replied, "I set her down on the other side, but you are still carrying her!"

Adapted from various versions on the internet

THE BRIDGE

This is a story of two brothers who lived side by side in their own farms for many years, until one day a foolish argument caused a rift between them. This was the first serious disagreement the brothers had in all of their 50 years. Up until that day, they always worked their fields together, shared knowledge and produce, and lent a helping hand to one another in times of need.

The fight began over a small misunderstanding, which can sometimes happen, but the dispute dragged on and became an angry exchange of words, followed by weeks of silence.

One day, there was a knock on the older brother's door. When he opened it, he was facing an old, bearded carpenter, holding a toolbox. "I could sure use some work, sir," said the stranger. "Do you need any repairs in your farm?" "Yes," replied the brother. "I've got a job for you. Across the creek, there's a farm that happens to belong to my younger brother. Until recently, the whole area between our homes was green, but then he changed the creek's path, making it into a border between us. I'm sure he did that out of spite, but I'll show him...," said the older brother. "You see those trees by the barn? I want you to turn them into a 10-foot tall fence. I never want to see his face again."

The old carpenter thought quietly to himself for a few minutes and eventually said: "I see."

The farmer helped the carpenter carry his tools and the wood, and then drove off to the city on some errands. When he came back in the evening, the old carpenter had finished.

Upon arriving at the creek, the older brother was stunned. His eyes bulged out, and he couldn't utter a single word. Where a fence should have been standing, a bridge now stood. A quaint and special bridge, truly a work of art, with an intricately carved banister.

At the same time, the younger brother happened to come to the same spot. He rushed over the bridge, embraced his older brother and said: "You're something special... building a bridge, after all I've said and done!"

While both brothers were hugging, the old carpenter collected his tools and started walking away. The brothers turned to him and said, "Please, stay for a few more days – we have more things that need fixing."

"I would have loved to stay, kind sirs," said the carpenter. "But I have many more bridges to build and things to fix in other places..."

The moral of our story is a simple one: we often let anger push us away from our loved ones, and allow pride to come before our love. Don't let it happen to you. Learn to forgive and appreciate what you have.

Remember: the past cannot be changed, but the future can be. No quarrel can spoil a true connection. Build your bridges when you have to, and always cross them with a smile.

Adapted from various versions on the internet

─────────── ■ ■ ■ ───────────

HOW THE BABEMBA TRIBE FORGIVES

In the Babemba tribe of Southern Africa, when a person acts irresponsibly or unjustly, he is placed in the centre of the village, alone and unfettered. All work ceases and every man, woman and child in the village gathers in a large circle around the accused individual.

Then each person in the tribe, regardless of age, speaks to the accused, one at a time. Each recalls the good things the person in the centre of the circle has done in his lifetime. Every incident, every experience that can be recalled with any detail and accuracy, is recounted. All his positive attributes, good deeds, strengths and kindnesses are recited carefully and at length.

This tribal ceremony continues until everyone in the village has his or her say about how they value this person as a respected member of their community, and it can last for several days. At the end, the tribal circle is broken, a joyous celebration takes place, and the person is symbolically and literally welcomed back into the tribe.

Author Unknown

DR WAYNE DYER (1940-2015)

Internationally renowned self-development author and speaker Dr Wayne Dyer had a deeply personal story on forgiveness. It led to an amazing shift in his life, as told on the Bonnie Hunt Show in America.

His father had abandoned him when he was an infant. Consequently, his mother, who was just twenty-two and had two other boys (all her sons were under the age of four), had to place them in foster homes. He grew up hating the father he never knew.

In 1974, Dr Dyer found out his father had been an alcoholic and, ten years ago, had died from cirrhosis of the liver. He decided to visit his father's grave in Biloxi, Mississippi and upon arriving, stood there for three hours. He stomped on the grave and was still angry, but in the last few minutes of his visit something came over him. He said to his father: "From this moment on I send you love, and I forgive you for everything that you have done." When he walked away from his father's grave that day, he said everything in his life started to change.

At the time he was overweight, drinking and was in a bad relationship. His writing was not doing what he wanted. But after this 'act of forgiveness' that helped him release a lifetime of anger and pain, Dr Dyer said his whole life took off. He wrote the book, Your Erroneous Zones, which became a worldwide best-seller. He stopped drinking and got back into shape. He also started attracting the right people into his life. Everything transformed when he forgave.

"He who seeks vengeance must dig two graves: one for his enemy and one for himself." Chinese Proverb

"Without forgiveness, the world is lost. It's like those two prisoners of war that met years later, and one said to the other, 'Have you forgiven your captors yet?' And the second one said, 'No, I never will.' And then the first one said, 'Well then, they still have you in prison, don't they?'"

■ ■ ■

DRIVE SAFELY

Jack took a look at his speedometer before slowing down; seventy-three in a fifty-five zone... the fourth time in as many months. How could a guy get caught so often? When his car had slowed to ten miles an hour, Jack pulled over, but only partially. Let the cop worry about the potential traffic hazard. Maybe some other car will tweak his backside with a mirror.

The cop was stepping out of his car, the big pad in hand. Bob? Bob from church? Jack sunk further into his trench coat. This was worse than the coming ticket. A Christian cop catching a guy from his own church. A guy who happened to be a little eager to get home after a long day at the office. A guy he was about to play golf with tomorrow. Jumping out of the car, he approached a man he saw every Sunday, a man he'd never seen in uniform.

"Hi, Bob. Fancy meeting you like this."

"Hello, Jack." No smile.

"Guess you caught me red-handed in a rush to see my wife and kids."

"Yeah, I guess."

Bob seemed uncertain. Good.

"I've seen some long days at the office lately. I'm afraid I bent the rules a bit, just this once." Jack toed at a pebble on the pavement. "Diane said something about roast beef and potatoes tonight. Know what I mean?"

"I know what you mean. I also know that you have a reputation in our precinct."

Ouch! This was not going in the right direction. Time to change tactics.

"What'd you clock me at?"

"Seventy-one. Would you sit back in your car, please?"

"Now wait a minute here, Bob. I checked as soon as I saw you. I was barely nudging sixty-five." The lie seemed to come easier with every ticket.

"Please, Jack, in the car."

Flustered, Jack hunched himself through the still-open door. Slamming it shut, he stared at the dashboard. He was in no rush to open the window. The minutes ticked by. Bob scribbled away on the pad. Why hadn't he asked for a driver's licence? Whatever the reason, it would be a month of Sundays before Jack ever sat near this cop again.

A tap on the door jerked his head to the left. There was Bob, a folded paper in hand. Jack rolled down the window a mere two inches, just enough room for Bob to pass him the slip.

"Thanks." Jack could not quite keep the sneer out of his voice.

Bob returned to his car without a word. Jack watched his retreat in the mirror and unfolded the sheet of paper. How much was this one going to cost?

Wait a minute. What was this? Some kind of joke? Certainly not a ticket. Jack began to read:

"Dear Jack,

Once upon a time I had a daughter. She was six when killed by a car. You guessed it - a speeding driver. A fine and three months in jail, and the man was free. Free to hug his daughters. All three of them. I only had one, and I'm going to have to wait until heaven before I can ever hug her again. A thousand times I've tried to forgive that man. A thousand times I thought I had. Maybe I did, but I need to do it again. Even now. Pray for me. And be careful. My son is all I have left.

Bob."

Jack twisted around in time to see Bob's car pull away and head down the road. He watched until it disappeared. A full fifteen minutes later, he, too, pulled away and drove slowly home, praying for forgiveness and hugging a surprised wife and kids when he arrived.

Author Unknown

CHAPTER EIGHT : FRIENDSHIP

WHOSE LIFE CAN YOU TOUCH TODAY?

When I was quite young, my father had one of the first telephones in our neighbourhood. I remember well the polished old case fastened to the wall. The shiny receiver hung on the side of the box. I was too little to reach the telephone, but used to listen with fascination when my mother talked to it. Then I discovered that somewhere inside this wonderful device lived an amazing person - her name was "Information, Please" and there was nothing she did not know. "Information, Please" could supply anybody's number and the correct time.

My first personal experience with this genie-in the-bottle came one day while my mother was visiting a neighbour. Amusing myself at the tool bench in the basement, I whacked my finger with a hammer. The pain was terrible but there didn't seem to be any reason to cry because there was no one home to give sympathy. I walked around the house sucking my throbbing finger, finally arriving at the stairway. The telephone! Quickly, I ran for the footstool in the parlour and dragged it to the landing. Climbing up, I unhooked the receiver and held it to my ear. "Information, Please," I said into the mouthpiece just above my head.

A click or two and a small, clear voice spoke into my ear, "Information."

"I hurt my finger," I wailed into the phone. The tears came readily enough now that I had an audience.

"Isn't your mother home?" came the question.

"Nobody's home but me," I blubbered.

"Are you bleeding?" the voice asked.

"No," I replied. "I hit my finger with the hammer and it hurts."

"Can you open your icebox?" she asked.

I said I could. "Then chip off a little piece of ice and hold it to your finger," said the voice.

After that, I called "Information, Please" for everything. I asked her for help with my geography and she told me where Philadelphia was. She helped me with my maths. She told me my pet chipmunk, which I had caught in the park just the day before, would eat fruit and nuts.

Then there was the time Petey, our pet canary, died. I called "Information, Please" and told her the sad story. She listened, and then said the usual things grown-ups say to soothe a child, but I was inconsolable. I asked her, "Why is it that birds should sing so beautifully and bring joy to all families, only to end up as a heap of feathers on the bottom of a cage?"

She must have sensed my deep concern, for she said quietly, "Paul, always remember that there are other worlds to sing in." Somehow I felt better.

Another day I was on the telephone. "Information, Please"

"Information," said the now familiar voice.

"How do you spell fix?" I asked.

All this took place in a small town in the Pacific Northwest. When I was nine years old, we moved across the country to Boston. I missed my friend very much. "Information, Please" belonged in that old wooden box back home, and I somehow never thought of trying the tall, shiny new phone that sat on the table in the hall.

As I grew into my teens, the memories of those childhood conversations never really left me. Often, in moments of doubt and perplexity, I would recall the serene sense of security I had then. I appreciated now how patient, understanding and kind she was to have spent her time on a little boy.

A few years later, on my way west to college, my plane put down in Seattle. I had about half an hour or so between planes. I spent 15 minutes on the phone with my sister, who lived there now. Then without thinking what I was doing, I dialled my hometown operator and said, "Information, Please." Miraculously, I heard the small, clear voice I knew so well. "Information."

I hadn't planned this but I heard myself saying, "Could you please tell me how to spell fix?"

There was a long pause. Then came the soft-spoken answer, "I guess your finger must have healed by now."

I laughed. "So it's really still you," I said. "I wonder if you have any idea how much you meant to me during that time?"

"I wonder," she said, "if you know how much your calls meant to me? I never had any children, and I used to look forward to your calls."

I told her how often I had thought of her over the years and I asked if I could call her again when I came back to visit my sister.

"Please do," she said. "Just ask for Sally."

Three months later I was back in Seattle. A different voice answered, "Information."

I asked for Sally.

"Are you a friend?" she asked.

"Yes, a very old friend," I answered.

"I'm sorry to have to tell you this," she said. "Sally has been working part-time the last few years because she was sick. She died five weeks ago."

Before I could hang up she said, "Wait a minute. Did you say your name was Paul?" "Yes," I replied.

"Well, Sally left a message for you. She wrote it down in case you called. Let me read it to you."

The note read: "Tell him I still say there are other worlds to sing in. He'll know what I mean."

I thanked her and hung up. I knew what Sally meant.

Author Unknown

THE BIG BLACK LABRADOR

They told me the big black Lab's name was Reggie, as I looked at him lying in his pen. The shelter was clean, no-kill and the people really friendly. I'd only been in the area for six months, but everywhere I went in the small college town, people were welcoming and open. Everyone waved when you passed them on the street. But something was still missing as I attempted to settle in to my new life here, and I thought a dog couldn't hurt. Give me someone to talk to.

And I had just seen Reggie's advertisement on the local news. The shelter said they had received numerous calls right after, but that the people who had come down to see him just didn't look like "Lab people," whatever that meant. They must've thought I did.

At first, I thought the shelter had misjudged me in giving me Reggie and his things, which consisted of a dog pad, bag of toys (almost all of which were brand new tennis balls), his dishes and a sealed letter from his previous owner. See, Reggie and I didn't really hit it off when we got home. We struggled for two weeks (which is how long the shelter told me to give him to adjust to his new home). Maybe it was the fact that I was trying to adjust, too. Maybe we were too much alike.

For some reason, his stuff (except for the tennis balls - he wouldn't go anywhere without two stuffed in his mouth) got tossed in with all of my other unpacked boxes. I guess I didn't really think he'd need all his old stuff, that I'd get him new things once he settled in. But it became pretty clear pretty soon that he wasn't going to.

I tried the normal commands the shelter told me he knew, ones like "sit" and "stay" and "come" and "heel", and he'd follow them - when he felt like it. He never really seemed to listen when I called his name; sure, he'd look in my direction after the fourth or fifth time I said it, but then he'd just go back to doing whatever. When I'd ask again, you could almost see him sigh and then grudgingly obey.

This just wasn't going to work. He chewed a couple of shoes and some unpacked boxes. I was a little too stern with him and he resented it, I could tell. The friction got so bad that I couldn't wait for the two weeks to be up, and when it was, I was in full-on search mode for my cell phone amid all of my unpacked stuff. I remembered leaving it on the stack of boxes for the guest room, but I also mumbled, rather cynically, that the "damn dog probably hid it from me."

Finally, I found it. But before I could punch in the shelter's number, I also found his pad and other toys from the shelter. I tossed the pad in Reggie's direction and he snuffed it and wagged, with the most enthusiasm I'd seen since bringing him home. But then I called, "Hey, Reggie, you like that? Come here and I'll give you a treat." Instead, he sort of glanced in my direction - maybe 'glared' is more accurate - and then gave a discontented sigh and flopped down... with his back to me.

Well, that's not going to do it either, I thought. And I punched the shelter phone number. But I hung up when I saw the sealed envelope. I had completely forgotten about that, too. "Okay, Reggie," I said out loud, "let's see if your previous owner has any advice."

The letter read:

Whoever Gets My Dog:

Well, I can't say that I'm happy you're reading this, a letter I told the shelter could only be opened by Reggie's new owner. I'm not even happy writing it. If you're reading this, it means I just got back from my last car ride with my Lab after dropping him off at the shelter. He knew something was different. I have packed up his pad and toys before and set them by the back door before a trip, but this time... it's like he knew something was wrong. And something is wrong...which is why I have to go to try to make it right.

So, let me tell you about my Lab in the hopes that it will help you bond with him and he with you. First, he loves tennis balls. The more the merrier. Sometimes I think he's part squirrel, the way he hordes them. He usually always has two in his mouth, and he tries to get a third in there. He hasn't done it yet. Doesn't matter where you throw them, he'll bound after it, so be careful - really, don't do it by any roads. I made that mistake once, and it almost cost him dearly.

Next, commands. Maybe the shelter staff already told you, but I'll go over them again: Reggie knows the obvious ones - "sit", "stay", "come" and "heel." He knows hand signals: "back" to turn around and go back when you put your hand straight up; and "over" if you put your hand out right or left. "Shake" for shaking water off and "paw" for a high-five. He does "down" when he feels like lying down - I bet you could work on that with him some more. He knows "ball" and "food" and "bone" and "treat", like nobody's business.

I trained Reggie with small food treats. Nothing opens his ears like little pieces of hot dog. Feeding schedule: twice a day, about seven in the morning, and again at six in the evening. Regular store-bought stuff; the shelter has the brand. He's up on his shots. Call the clinic on 9th Street and update his info with yours; they'll make sure to send you reminders for when he's due. Be forewarned: Reggie hates the vet. Good luck getting him in the car. I don't know how he knows when it's time to go to the vet, but he knows.

Finally, give him some time. I've never been married, so it's only been Reggie and me for his whole life. He's gone everywhere with me, so please include him on your daily car rides if you can. He sits well in the backseat, and he doesn't bark or complain. He just loves to be around people and me most especially. Which means that this transition is going to be hard, with him going to live with someone new? And that's why I need to share one more bit of info with you... His name's not Reggie. I don't know what made me do it, but when I dropped him off at the shelter, I told them his name was Reggie. He's a smart dog, he'll get used to it and will respond to it, of that I have no doubt. But I just couldn't bear to give them his real name. For me to do that, it seemed so final, that handing him over to the shelter was as good as me admitting that I'd never see him again. And if I end up coming back, getting him, and tearing up this letter, it means everything's fine. But if someone else is reading it, well ... well it means that his new owner should know his real name. It'll help you bond with him. Who knows, maybe you'll even notice a change in his demeanour if he's been giving you problems. His real name is "Tank".

Because that is what I drive. Again, if you're reading this and you're from the area, maybe my name has been on the news. I told the shelter that they couldn't make "Reggie" available for adoption until they received word from my company commander. See, my parents are gone, I have no siblings, no one I could've left Tank with ... and it was my only real request of the Army upon my deployment to Iraq; that they make one phone call the shelter ... in the "event" ... to tell them that Tank could be put up for adoption. Luckily, my colonel is a dog guy too, and he knew where my platoon was headed. He said he'd do it personally. And if you're reading this, then he made good on his word.

Well, this letter is getting downright depressing, even though, frankly, I'm just writing it for my dog. I couldn't imagine if I was writing it for a wife and kids and family ...but still, Tank has been my family for the last six years, almost as long as the Army has been my family. And now I hope and pray that you make him part of your family and that he will adjust and come to love you the same way he loved me.

That unconditional love from a dog is what I take with me to Iraq as an inspiration to do something selfless, to protect innocent people from those who would do terrible things ... and to keep those terrible people from coming over here. If I have to give up Tank in order to do it, I am glad to have done so. He is my example of service and of love. I hope I honoured him by my service to my country and comrades.

All right, that's enough. I deploy this evening and have to drop this letter off at the shelter. I don't think I'll say another good-bye to Tank, though. I cried too much the first time. Maybe I'll peek in on him and see if he finally got that third tennis ball in his mouth.

Good luck with Tank. Give him a good home, and give him an extra kiss goodnight - every night - from me.

Thank you,

Paul Mallory

I folded the letter and slipped it back in the envelope. Sure, I had heard of Paul Mallory, everyone in town knew him, even new people like me. Local kid, killed in Iraq a few months ago and posthumously earning the Silver Star when he gave his life to save three buddies. Flags had been at half-mast all summer.

I leaned forward in my chair and rested my elbows on my knees, staring at the dog. "Hey, Tank," I said quietly. The dog's head whipped up, his ears cocked and his eyes bright. "C 'mere, boy." He was instantly on his feet, his nails clicking on the hardwood floor. He sat in front of me, his head tilted; searching for the name he hadn't heard in months. "Tank," I whispered. His tail swished.

I kept whispering his name, over and over, and each time, his ears lowered, his eyes softened and his posture relaxed as a wave of contentment just seemed to flood him. I stroked his ears, rubbed his shoulders, buried my face into his scruff and hugged him.

"It's me now, Tank, just you and me. Your old pal gave you to me." Tank reached up and licked my cheek. "So whaddaya say we play some ball?" His ears perked again. "Yeah? Ball? You like that? Ball?" Tank tore from my hands and disappeared in the next room.

And when he came back, he had three tennis balls in his mouth.

Adapted from various versions on the internet

GENGHIS KHAN AND HIS FALCON

On a recent visit to Kazakhstan, in Central Asia, I had the chance to accompany some hunters who still use the falcon as a weapon. I don't want to get into a discussion here about the word 'hunt', except to say that, in this case, Nature was simply following its course.

I had no interpreter with me, but what could have been a problem turned out to be a blessing. Unable to talk to them, I paid more attention to what they were doing. Our small party stopped, and the man with the falcon on his arm remained a little way apart from us and removed the small silver hood from the bird's head. I don't know why he decided to stop just there, and I had no way of asking.

The bird took off, circled a few times, and then dived straight down towards the ravine, and stayed there. When we got close, we found a vixen caught in the bird's talons. That scene was repeated once more during the morning.

Back at the village, I met the people who were waiting for me and asked them how they managed to train the falcon to do everything I had seen it do, even to sit meekly on its owner's arm (and on mine too; they put some leather armbands on me and I could see the bird's sharp talons close up.)

It was a pointless question. No one had an explanation. They said that the art is passed from generation to generation – father trains son, and so on. But what will remain engraved in my mind forever are the snowy mountains in the background, the silhouetted figures of horse and horseman, the falcon leaving the horseman's arm, and that deadly dive.

What also remains is a story that one of those people told me while we were having lunch:

One morning, the Mongol warrior, Genghis Khan, and his court went out hunting. His companions carried bows and arrows, but Genghis Khan carried on his arm his favourite falcon, which was better and surer than any arrow, because it could fly into the skies and see everything that a human being could not.

However, despite the group's enthusiastic efforts, they found nothing. Disappointed, Genghis Khan returned to the encampment and in order not to take out his frustration on his companions, he left the rest of the party and rode on alone. They had stayed in the forest for longer than expected, and Khan was desperately tired and thirsty. In the summer heat, all the streams had dried up, and he could find nothing to drink. Then, to his amazement, he saw a thread of water flowing from a rock just in front of him.

He removed the falcon from his arm and took out the silver cup which he always carried with him. It was very slow to fill and, just as he was about to raise it to his lips, the falcon flew up, plucked the cup from his hands and dashed it to the ground.

Genghis Khan was furious. But then, the falcon was his favourite and perhaps it, too, was thirsty. He picked up the cup, cleaned off the dirt, and filled it again. When the cup was only half-empty this time, the falcon again attacked it, spilling the water.

Genghis Khan adored his bird, but he knew that he could not, under any circumstances, allow such disrespect; someone might be watching this scene from afar and, later on, would tell his warriors that the great conqueror was incapable of taming a mere bird.

This time, he drew his sword, picked up the cup and refilled it, keeping one eye on the stream and the other on the falcon. As soon as he had enough water in the cup and was ready to drink, the falcon again took flight and flew towards him. Khan, with one thrust, pierced the bird's breast.

The thread of water, however, had dried up; Khan determined how to find something to drink and climbed the rock in search of the spring. To his surprise, there really was a pool of water and, in the middle of it, dead, lay one of the most poisonous snakes in the region. If he had drunk the water, he, too, would have died.

Khan returned to camp with the dead falcon in his arms. He ordered a gold figurine of the bird to be made and on one of the wings, he had engraved:

"Even when a friend does something you do not like, he continues to be your friend."

And on the other wing, he had these words engraved:

"Any action committed in anger is an action doomed to failure."

A story by Paulo Coelho in 'Like the Flowing River'

A SIMPLE GESTURE

Mark was walking home from school one day when he noticed the boy ahead of him had tripped and dropped all of the books he was carrying, along with two sweaters, a baseball bat, a glove and a small tape recorder.

Mark knelt down and helped the boy pick up the scattered articles. Since they were going the same way, he helped to carry part of the burden. As they walked, Mark discovered the boy's name was Bill, that he loved video games, baseball and history, that he was having lots of trouble with his other subjects and that he had just broken up with his girlfriend.

They arrived at Bill's home first and Mark was invited in for a Coke and to watch some television. The afternoon passed pleasantly with a few laughs and some shared small talk, then Mark went home.

They continued to see each other around school, had lunch together once or twice, and then both graduated from junior high school. They ended up in the same high school where they had brief contacts over the years.

Finally, the long-awaited senior year came and three weeks before graduation, Bill asked Mark if they could talk. Bill reminded him of the day, years ago, when they had first met. "Did you ever wonder why I was carrying so many things home that day?" asked Bill.

"You see, I cleaned out my locker because I didn't want to leave a mess for anyone else. I had stored away some of my mother's sleeping pills and I was going home to commit suicide. But after we spent some time together talking and laughing, I realised that if I had killed myself, I would have missed that time and so many others that might follow.

So, you see, Mark, when you picked up those books that day, you did a lot more. You saved my life."

A true story by John W. Schlatter,
adapted from various versions on the internet

SHAYA PLAYS BASEBALL

In Brooklyn, New York, Chush is a school that caters for children with learning disabilities. Some children remain in Chush for their entire school career while others can transfer into conventional schools. At a Chush fund-raising dinner, the father of a Chush child delivered a speech that will always be remembered by all who attended.

After extolling the school and its dedicated staff, he cried out, "Where is the perfection in my son Shaya? Everything Nature does is done with perfection. But my son, Shaya, cannot learn things as other children do. He cannot remember facts and figures as other children do. Where is Nature's perfection?"

The audience was stilled by the question, and pained by the father's anguish.

"I believe," the father continued, "that when a child like Shaya comes into this world, an opportunity to realise true human nature presents itself, and it comes in the way other people treat that child."

He then told the following story about his son Shaya:

One afternoon, Shaya and his father walked past a park where some boys whom Shaya knew were playing baseball. Shaya asked, "Do you think they will let me play?"

Shaya's father knew that his son was not at all athletic and that most boys would not want him on their team. But Shaya's father also understood that if his son was chosen to play it would give him a comfortable sense of belonging. Shaya's father approached one of the boys in the field and asked if Shaya could play. The boy looked around for guidance from his team mates. Getting none, he took matters into his own hands and said, "We are losing by six runs and the game is in the eighth inning. I guess he can be on our team and we'll try to put him up to bat in the ninth inning."

Shaya's father was ecstatic as Shaya smiled broadly. Shaya was told to put on a glove and go out to play short centre field. In the bottom of the eighth inning, Shaya's team scored a few runs but was still behind by three. In the bottom of the ninth inning, Shaya's team scored again and now, with two outs and the bases loaded with the potential winning run on base, Shaya was scheduled to be up. Would the team actually let Shaya bat at this juncture and give away their chance to win the game?

Surprisingly, Shaya was given the bat. Everyone knew that it was all but impossible because Shaya didn't even know how to hold the bat properly, let alone hit with it.

However, as Shaya stepped up to the plate, the pitcher moved a few steps to lob the ball in softly so Shaya should at least be able to make contact. The first pitch came and Shaya swung clumsily and missed. One of Shaya's team mates came up to Shaya and together they held the bat and faced the pitcher waiting for the next pitch.

The pitcher again took a few steps forward to toss the ball softly toward Shaya. As the pitch came in, Shaya and his team mate swung at the ball and together they hit a slow ground ball to the pitcher. The pitcher picked up the soft grounder and could easily have thrown the ball to the first baseman. Shaya would have been out and that would have ended the game.

Instead, the pitcher took the ball and threw it on a high arc to right field, far beyond reach of the first baseman. Everyone started yelling, "Shaya, run to first. Run to first!" Never in his life had Shaya run to first and he scampered down the baseline wide eyed and startled. By the time he reached first base, the right fielder had the ball. He could have thrown the ball to the second baseman, who would tag out the still-running Shaya.

But the right fielder understood what the pitcher's intentions were so he threw the ball high and far over the third baseman's head. Everyone yelled, "Run to second, run to second!" Shaya ran towards second base as the runners ahead of him deliriously circled the bases towards home. As Shaya reached second base, the opposing short stop ran to him, turned him in the direction of third base and shouted, "Run to third!" As Shaya rounded third, the boys from both teams ran behind him screaming, "Shaya, run home!" Shaya ran home, stepped on home plate and all 18 boys lifted him on their shoulders and made him the hero. He had just hit a "grand slam" and won the game for his team.

"That day," said the father softly, with tears now rolling down his face, "those 18 boys from both teams helped bring friendship and a piece of true love and humanity into the world."

From 'Echoes of the Maggid' by Rabbi Paysach Krohn, told to him by Shaya's father.

CHAPTER NINE :
HAPPINESS

THE TAIL OF HAPPINESS

This story begins in an alleyway, where a little kitten can be seen vigorously chasing its tail.

The kitten is using all of its efforts to catch its tail with its mouth; running in circles, again and again, believing it is getting closer to snatching up its tail. Watching from a distance is an older, rough-looking alley cat, who is wondering what the little kitten is doing.

The older alley cat approaches the little kitten and asks, "What are you up to, little kitten?" The kitten then replies, "I am chasing my tail!"

"Why is it that you are chasing your tail and why are you so determined to get a hold of it?"

The little kitten replies to the alley cat with a very simple answer - and a good reason. "I just came back from cat philosophy school and I was taught that the most important thing for us cats is happiness. I have learnt that the source of this happiness is in our tails, so once I get a firm grasp on it, I can always have the thing that is most important to me: happiness!"

The old alley cat is taken back by the kitten's answer and simply smiles, then adds to the little kitten's insight by saying, "Well, little kitten, I am much older than you and I have not had the same opportunity as you had to attend cat philosophy school. I have been living in these alleys and streets for many years and it has been rough. I have to constantly search for food and shelter, while facing tough competition.

My time in these alleys has taught me much though. I have also learnt that the most important thing to us cats is happiness - and the source of this happiness is indeed in our tails. But there is something that I have learnt that you, little kitten, have not yet witnessed."

"What is that?" the little kitten asks.

"I have learnt that if I live my life the way I want to live it each day and go on about my business, happiness follows me wherever I go..."

A story narrated in a lecture by Dr Wayne Dyer

JOHN LENNON (1940-1980)

"When I was five years old my mother always told me that happiness was the key to life. When I went to school, they asked me what I wanted to be when I grew up. I wrote down 'happy'. They told me I didn't understand the assignment, and I told them they didn't understand life!"

John Lennon, English singer, songwriter and peace activist, who co-founded The Beatles.

ADVICE FROM ROSE

The first day of school our professor introduced himself and challenged us to get to know someone we didn't already know. I stood up to look around when a gentle hand touched my shoulder. I turned around to find a wrinkled, little old lady beaming up at me with a smile that lit up her entire being. "Hi handsome. My name is Rose. I'm eighty-seven years old. Can I give you a hug?" she said. I laughed and enthusiastically responded, "Of course you may!" and she gave me a giant squeeze.

"Why are you in college at such a young, innocent age?" I asked. She jokingly replied, "I'm here to meet a rich husband, get married, have a couple of children and then retire and travel." "No, seriously," I asked. I was curious what may have motivated her to be taking on this challenge at her age. "I always dreamed of having a college education and now I'm getting one!" she told me.

After class we walked to the student union building and shared a chocolate milkshake. We became instant friends. Every day for the next three months we would leave class together and talk nonstop. I was always mesmerised listening to this 'time machine', as she shared her wisdom and experience with me.

Over the course of the year, Rose became a campus icon and she easily made friends wherever she went. She loved to dress up and she revelled in the attention bestowed upon her from the other students. She was living it up. At the end of the semester we invited Rose to speak at our football banquet. I'll never forget what she taught us. She was introduced and stepped up to the podium. As she began to

112

deliver her prepared speech, she dropped her three-by-five cards on the floor. Frustrated and a little embarrassed, she leaned into the microphone and simply said, "I'm sorry I'm so jittery. I gave up beer for Lent and this whiskey is killing me! I'll never get my speech back in order so let me just tell you what I know." As we laughed, she cleared her throat and began:

"We do not stop playing because we are old; we grow old because we stop playing. There are only four secrets to staying young, being happy and achieving success. Firstly, you have to laugh and find humour every day. Secondly, you've got to have a dream. When you lose your dreams, you die. We have so many people walking around who are dead and don't even know it! Then, there is a huge difference between growing older and growing up. If you are nineteen years old and lie in bed for one full year and don't do one productive thing, you will turn twenty years old. If I am eighty-seven years old and stay in bed for a year and never do anything I will turn eighty-eight. Anybody can grow older. That doesn't take any talent or ability. The idea is to grow up by always finding the opportunity in change. And lastly, have no regrets. The elderly usually don't have regrets for what we did, but rather for things we did not do. The only people who fear death are those with regrets."

She concluded her speech by courageously singing Bette Midler's The Rose. She challenged each of us to study the lyrics and live them out in our daily lives.

At the year's end, Rose finished the college degree she had begun all those years ago. One week after graduation, she died peacefully in her sleep. More than two thousand college students attended her funeral in tribute to the wonderful woman who taught by example that it's never too late to be all you can possibly be.

Remember; GROWING OLDER IS MANDATORY, GROWING UP IS OPTIONAL.

Life is 10% what happens to me and 90% how I react to it.

Adapted from various versions on the internet

———————————— ▪ ▪ ▪ ————————————

GRATITUDE

It's not happiness that brings us gratitude. It's gratitude that brings us happiness.

If you have food in your fridge, clothes on your back, a roof overhead and a place to sleep, you are richer than 75 percent of this world

If you woke up this morning with more health than illness, you are more blessed than the million who will not survive this week.

If you have money in the bank, in your wallet, and spare change in a dish or moneybox someplace, you are among the top 8 percent of the world's wealthy.

If you can attend a church meeting or service without fear of harassment, arrest, torture, or death, you are more blessed than three billion people in the world.

If you have never experienced the danger of battle, the loneliness of imprisonment, the agony of torture, or the pangs of starvation, you are ahead of 500 million people in the world.

If you hold up your head with a smile on your face and are truly thankful, you are blessed because the majority can, but most do not.

And if you can read this message, you are more blessed than more than two billion people in the world who cannot read at all.

Author Unknown

DEAR STRANGER

A Letter on the Subject of Happiness

Dear Stranger,

You don't know me but I hear you are going through a tough time, and I would like to help you. I want to be open and honest with you, and let you know that happiness isn't something just afforded to a special few. It can be yours, if you take the time to let it grow.

It's OK to be stressed, scared and sad. I certainly have been throughout my 66 years. I've confronted my biggest fears time and time again. I've cheated death on many adventures, seen loved ones pass away, failed in business, minced my words in front of tough audiences and had my heart broken.

I know I'm fortunate to live an extraordinary life, and that most people would assume my business success, and the wealth that comes with it, have brought me happiness. But they haven't; in fact, it's the reverse. I am successful, wealthy and connected because I am happy.

So many people get caught up in doing what they think will make them happy but, in my opinion, this is where they fail. Happiness is not about doing, it's about being. In order to be happy, you need to think consciously about it. Don't forget the to-do list, but remember to write a 'to-be' list too.

Kids are often asked: 'What do you want to be when you grow up?' The world expects grandiose aspirations: 'I want to be a writer, a doctor, the prime minister.' They're told: 'go to school, go to college, get a job, get married, and then you'll

116

be happy'. But that's all about doing, not being – and while doing will bring you moments of joy, it won't necessarily reward you with lasting happiness.

Stop and breathe. Be healthy. Be around your friends and family. Be there for someone, and let someone be there for you. Be bold. Just be for a minute.

If you allow yourself to be in the moment, and appreciate the moment, happiness will follow. I speak from experience. We've built a business empire, joined conversations about the future of our planet, attended many memorable parties and met many unforgettable people. And while these things have brought me great joy, it's the moments that I stopped just to be, rather than do, that have given me true happiness. Why? Because allowing yourself just to be, puts things into perspective. Try it. Be still. Be present.

For me, it's watching the flamingos fly across Necker Island at dusk. It's holding my new grandchild's tiny hands. It's looking up at the stars and dreaming of seeing them up close one day. It's listening to my family's dinner-time debates. It's the smile on a stranger's face, the smell of rain, the ripple of a wave, the wind across the sand. It's the first snow fall of winter, and the last storm of summer. It's sunrise and sunset.

There's a reason we're called human beings and not human doings. As human beings we have the ability to think, move and communicate in a heightened way. We can cooperate, understand, reconcile and love...that's what sets us apart from most other species.

Don't waste your human talents by stressing about nominal things, or that which you cannot change. If you take the time simply to be and appreciate the fruits of life, your stresses will begin to dissolve, and you will be happier.

But don't just seek happiness when you're down. Happiness shouldn't be a goal, it should be a habit. Take the focus off doing, and start being every day. Be loving, be grateful, be helpful, and be a spectator to your own thoughts.

Allow yourself to be in the moment, and appreciate the moment. Take the focus off everything you think you need to do and start being – I promise you, happiness will follow.

Happy regards,

Richard Branson

Posted on the virgin.com website

------------------------ ■ ■ ■ ------------------------

BLISS

A Sufi mystic had remained happy his whole life; no one had ever seen him unhappy. He was always laughing, he was laughter, and his whole being was a perfume of celebration...

In his old age, when he was dying, on his deathbed and still enjoying death, laughing hilariously, a disciple asked, "You puzzle us. Now you are dying, why are you laughing? What is there about it? We are feeling so sad. We wanted to ask you many times in your life why you are never sad. But now, confronting death at least, one should be sad. You are still laughing – how do you manage it?"

The old man said, "It is simple; I had asked my master. I had gone to my master as a young man; I was only seventeen and already miserable, and my master was old, seventy, and he was sitting under a tree, laughing for no reason at all. There was nobody else there, nothing had happened, nobody had cracked a joke or anything, and he was simply laughing, holding his belly. I asked him, 'What is the matter with you? Are you mad or something?'

He said, 'One day I was also as sad as you are. Then it dawned on me that it is my choice, it is my life. Since that day, every morning when I get up, the first thing I decide is... before I open my eyes I say to myself, 'Abdullah' - that was his name - 'what do you want? Misery? Blissfulness? What you are going to choose today?' And it happens that I always choose blissfulness.

"'It is a choice. Try it. When you become aware the first moment in the morning that sleep has left, ask yourself, 'Abdullah, another day! What is your idea? Do you choose misery or blissfulness?

"'And who would choose misery? And why? It is so unnatural — unless one feels blissful in misery, but then too you are choosing bliss, not misery!'"

A Sufi story

THE ALPHABET OF HAPPINESS

A - *ACCEPT*
Accept others for who they are and for the choices they've made, even if you have difficulty understanding their beliefs, motives or actions.

B - *BREAK AWAY*
Break away from everything that stands in the way of what you hope to accomplish in your life.

C - *CREATE*
Create a family of friends with whom you can share your hopes, dreams, sorrows and happiness.

D - *DECIDE*
Decide that you'll be successful and happy come what may, and good things will find you. The roadblocks are only minor obstacles along the way.

E - *EXPLORE*
Explore and experiment. The world has much to offer, and you have much to give. And every time you try something new, you'll learn more about yourself.

F - *FORGIVE*
Forgive and forget. Grudges only weigh you down and inspire unhappiness and grief. Soar above it, and remember that everyone makes mistakes.

G - *GROW*
Leave the childhood monsters behind. They can no longer hurt you or stand in your way.

H - *HOPE*
Hope for the best and never forget that anything is possible as long as you remain dedicated to the task.

I - *IGNORE*
Ignore the negative voice inside your head. Focus instead on your goals and remember your accomplishments. Your past success is only a small inkling of what the future holds.

J - *JOURNEY*
Journey to new worlds, new possibilities, by remaining open-minded. Try to learn something new every day, and you'll grow.

K - *KNOW*
Know that no matter how bad things seem, they'll always get better. The warmth of spring always follows the harshest of winters.

L - *LOVE*
Let love fill your heart instead of hate. When hate is in your heart, there's room for nothing else, but when love is in your heart, there's room for endless happiness.

M - *MANAGE*
Manage your time and your expenses wisely, and you'll suffer less stress and worry. Then you'll be able to focus on the important things in life.

N – *NOTICE*
Never ignore the poor, infirm, helpless, weak, or suffering. Offer your assistance when possible, and always offer your kindness and understanding.

O – *OPEN.*
Open your eyes and take in all the beauty around you. Even during the worst of times, there's still much to be thankful for.

P – *PLAY*
Never forget to have fun along the way. Success means nothing without happiness.

Q – *QUESTION*
Ask many questions, because you're here to learn.

R – *RELAX*
Refuse to let worry and stress rule your life, and remember that things always have a way of working out in the end.

S – *SHARE*
Share your talent, skills, knowledge and time with others. Everything that you invest in others will return to you many times over.

T – *TRY*
Even when your dreams seem impossible to reach, try anyway. You'll be amazed by what you can accomplish.

U – *USE*
Use your gifts to your best ability. Talent that's wasted has no value. Talent that's used will bring unexpected rewards.

V – *VALUE*
Value the friends and family members who've supported and encouraged you, and be there for them as well.

W – *WORK*
Work hard every day to be the best person you can be, but never feel guilty if you fall short of your goals. Every sunrise offers a second chance.

X – *X-RAY*
Look deep inside the hearts of those around you and you'll see the goodness and beauty within.

Y – *YIELD to commitment*
If you stay on track and remain dedicated, you'll find success at the end of the road.

Z – ZOOM
Zoom to a happy place when bad memories or sorrow rear their ugly head. Let nothing interfere with your goals. Instead, focus on your abilities, your dreams, and a brighter tomorrow.

Author Unknown

CHAPTER TEN :
IMAGINATION

THE POODLE AND THE LEOPARD

A wealthy lady decides to go on a photo safari in Africa, taking her faithful aged poodle along for company. One day the poodle starts chasing butterflies and before long, he discovers that he's lost. Wandering about, he notices a hungry-looking leopard heading rapidly in his direction.

The old poodle thinks, "Oh, oh! I'm in deep doo-doo now!" Noticing some bones on the ground close by, he immediately settles down to chew on the bones with his back to the approaching cat. Just as the leopard is about to leap, the old poodle exclaims loudly, "Boy, that was one delicious leopard! I wonder if there are any more around here."

On hearing this, the young leopard halts his attack in mid-strike. A look of terror comes over him and he slinks away into the trees. "Whew!" says the leopard, "That was close! That old poodle nearly had me!"

Meanwhile, a monkey who had been watching the whole scene from a nearby tree, figures he can put this knowledge to good use and trade it for protection from the leopard. The old poodle sees the monkey heading after the leopard, and figures that something must be up. The monkey soon catches up with the leopard, spills the beans, and strikes a deal for himself with the leopard.

The young leopard is furious at being made a fool of and says, "Here, monkey, hop on my back and see what's going to happen to that conniving canine!"

Now, the old poodle sees the leopard coming with the monkey on his back and thinks, "What am I going to do now?" But instead of running, the dog sits down with his back to his attackers, pretending he hasn't seen them yet. Just when they get close enough to hear, the old poodle says, "Where's that darn monkey? I sent him off an hour ago to bring me another leopard!"

Adapted from various versions on the internet

THINKING OUT OF THE BOX

Many years ago, in a small Indian village, a farmer had the misfortune of owing a large sum of money to a village moneylender. The moneylender, who was old and ugly, fancied the farmer's beautiful daughter. So, he proposed a bargain.

He said he would forgo the farmer's debt if he could marry his daughter. Both the farmer and his daughter were horrified by the proposal. So the cunning moneylender suggested that they let providence decide the matter. He told them that he would put a black pebble and a white pebble into an empty money bag. Then the girl would have to pick one pebble from the bag.

If she picked the black pebble, she would become his wife and her father's debt would be forgiven.

If she picked the white pebble, she need not marry him and her father's debt would still be forgiven.

If she refused to pick a pebble, her father would be thrown into jail.

They were standing on a pebble strewn path in the farmer's field. As they talked, the moneylender bent over to pick up two pebbles. As he picked them up, the sharp-eyed girl noticed that he had picked up two black pebbles and put them into the bag. He then asked the girl to pick a pebble from the bag.

The girl put her hand into the moneybag and drew out a pebble. Without looking at it, she fumbled and let it fall onto the pebble-strewn path where it immediately became lost among all the other pebbles.

'Oh, how clumsy of me,' she said. 'But never mind. If you look into the bag for the one that is left, you will be able to tell which pebble I picked.'

Since the remaining pebble is black, it must be assumed that she had picked the white one. And since the moneylender dared not admit his dishonesty, the girl changed what seemed an impossible situation into an extremely advantageous one.

Adapted from various versions on the internet

———————————————— ▪ ▪ ▪ ————————————————

YOU CAN ALWAYS FIND A WAY

An old Italian gentleman lived alone in New Jersey. He wanted to plant his annual tomato garden, but it was very difficult work, as the ground was hard. His only son, Vincent, who would have helped him, was in prison. The old man wrote a letter to his son and described his predicament:

Dear Vincent,

I am feeling pretty sad because it looks like I won't be able to plant my tomato garden this year. I'm just getting too old to be digging up a garden plot. I know if you were here my troubles would be over. I know you would be happy to dig the plot for me, like in the old days.

Love, Papa

A few days later he received a letter from his son.

Dear Papa,

Don't dig up that garden. That's where the bodies are buried.

Love, Vinnie

At 4 am the next morning, FBI agents and local police arrived and dug up the entire area without finding any bodies. They apologised to the old man and left. That same day the old man received another letter from his son.

Dear Papa,

Go ahead and plant the tomatoes now. That's the best I could do under the circumstances.

Love you, Vinnie

Adapted from various versions on the internet

THE VIEW

Two men, both seriously ill, occupied the same hospital room. One man was allowed to sit up in his bed for an hour each afternoon to help drain the fluid from his lungs. His bed was next to the room's only window. The other man had to spend all his time flat on his back. The men talked for hours on end.

They spoke of their wives and their families, their homes, their jobs, their involvement in the military service, where they had been on vacation. Every afternoon when the man in the bed by the window could sit up, he would pass the time by describing to his roommate all the things he could see outside the window. The man in the other bed began to live for those one-hour periods where his world would be broadened and enlivened by all the activity and colour of the world outside.

The window overlooked a park with a lovely lake. Ducks and swans played on the water while children sailed their model boats. Young lovers walked arm in arm amidst flowers of every colour and a fine view of the city skyline could be seen in the distance. As the man by the window described all this in exquisite detail, the man on the other side of the room would close his eyes and imagine the picturesque scene.

One warm afternoon the man by the window described a parade passing by. Although the other man couldn't hear the band, he could see it in his mind's eye as the gentleman by the window portrayed it with descriptive words.

Days and weeks passed. One morning, the day nurse arrived to bring water for their baths, only to find the lifeless body of the man by the window, who had died peacefully in his sleep. She was saddened and called the hospital attendants to take the body away. As soon as it seemed appropriate, the other man asked if he could be moved next to the window. The nurse was happy to make the switch, and after making sure he was comfortable, she left him alone.

Slowly, painfully, he propped himself up on one elbow to take his first look at the real world outside. He strained to slowly turn to look out the window beside the bed. It faced a blank wall.

The man asked the nurse what could have compelled the deceased roommate to describe such wonderful things outside this window. The nurse responded that the man was blind and could not even see the wall. She said, "Perhaps he just wanted to encourage you?"

Adapted from various versions on the internet

WHY DOGS LIVE LESS THAN HUMANS

Being a vet, I had been called to examine a ten-year-old Irish Wolfhound named Belker. The dog's owners - Ron, his wife, Lisa and their little boy, Shane - were all very attached to Belker and they were hoping for a miracle.

I examined Belker and found he was dying. I told the family we couldn't do anything for Belker and offered to perform the euthanasia procedure for the old dog in their home.

129

As we made the arrangements, Ron and Lisa told me they thought it would be good for six-year-old Shane to observe the procedure. They felt as though Shane might learn something from the experience.

The next day, I felt the familiar catch in my throat as Belker's family surrounded him. Shane seemed so calm, petting the old dog for the last time, that I wondered if he understood what was going on. Within a few minutes, Belker slipped peacefully away.

The little boy seemed to accept Belker's transition without any difficulty or confusion. We sat together for a while after Belker's death, wondering aloud about the sad fact that animal lives are shorter than human lives. Shane, who had been listening quietly, piped up, "I know why."

Startled, we all turned to him. What came out of his mouth next stunned me. I'd never heard a more comforting explanation.

He said: "People are born so that they can learn how to live a good life — like loving everybody all the time and being nice, right?" The six-year-old continued, "Well, dogs already know how to do that, so they don't have to stay as long."

Author Unknown

SELF APPRAISAL

A little boy went into a drug store, reached for a soda carton and pulled it over to the telephone. He climbed onto the carton so that he could reach the buttons on the phone and proceeded to punch in ten-digits.

The store owner listened to the conversation:

Boy: 'Lady, can you give me the job of cutting your lawn?'

Woman (at the other end of the phone line): 'I already have someone to cut my lawn.'

Boy: 'Lady, I will cut your lawn for half the price of the person who cuts your lawn now.'

Woman: 'I'm very satisfied with the person who is presently cutting my lawn.'

Boy (with more perseverance): 'I'll even sweep your curb and your sidewalk, so on Sunday you will have the prettiest lawn in all of Palm beach, Florida.'

Woman: 'No, thank you.'

With a smile on his face, the little boy replaced the receiver. The store-owner, who was listening to all this, walked over to the boy.

Store Owner: 'Son... I like your attitude; I like that positive spirit and would like to offer you a job.'

Boy: 'Oh, no thanks.'

Store Owner: 'But you were really pleading for one.'

Boy: 'No Sir, I was just checking my performance at the job I already have. I am the one who is working for that lady I was talking to!'

Author unknown

131

CHAPTER ELEVEN : INTEGRITY

THE FLAT TYRE

There's a story of four college students who stayed out too late the night before a midterm chemistry exam and missed their early morning class the next day. The young men realising they'd missed the test and knew they had to come up with something fast for why they were late.

So they rushed in to see the professor and told him they had suffered a flat tyre on their way to the class and pleaded for the opportunity to take the exam the next day. To their astonishment, the professor gleefully agreed.

"Sure," he said, "Meet me here tomorrow and, because of your unfortunate circumstances, I'll allow you to take the exam."

Off they went, kicking their heels that the ploy had worked. They then studied all evening for the upcoming test. The next morning when they arrived, the professor asked them to each go to a different room and then he would provide them with the test.

The test had only one question: 'Which tyre was flat?'

Adapted from various versions on the internet

MYSELF

I have to live with myself and so
I want to be fit for myself to know.
I want to be able as days go by,
Always to look myself straight in the eye;
I don't want to stand with the setting sun
And hate myself for the things I have done.
I don't want to keep on a closet shelf
A lot of secrets about myself
And fool myself as I come and go
Into thinking no one else will ever know
The kind of person I really am,
I don't want to dress up myself in sham.
I want to go out with my head erect
I want to deserve all men's respect;
But here in the struggle for fame and wealth
I want to be able to like myself.
I don't want to look at myself and know that
I am bluster and bluff and empty show.
I never can hide myself from me;
I see what others may never see;
I know what others may never know,
I never can fool myself and so,
Whatever happens, I want to be
Self-respecting and conscience free.

By Edgar Albert Guest

THE COLLEGE APPLICATION

A young girl was filling out an application for college when she came across the question: 'Are you a leader?'

She thought for a moment and then decided that she had better be totally honest. Her answer was "No."

She was afraid that because of her answer, the college would reject her application. However, one month later she received a letter back from the college that read:

"Dear Candidate,

We would like to inform you that this year we have already reviewed more than a thousand applications. To date, there will be some 1,322 new leaders attending our program next year.

We are in the pleasant position to inform you that we have accepted your application because we felt it was imperative that all the leaders have at least one follower."

Author Unknown

A TEST

He stood up from the bench, straightened his Army uniform, and studied the crowd of people making their way through Grand Central Station.

He looked for the girl whose heart he knew, but whose face he didn't, the girl with the rose. His interest in her had begun 13 months before in a Florida Library. Taking a book off the shelf he found himself intrigued, not with the words of the book, but with the notes pencilled in the margin.

The soft handwriting reflected a thoughtful soul and insightful mind. In the front of the book, he discovered the previous owner's name, Miss Hollis Maynell.

With time and effort, he located her address. She lived in New York City. He wrote her a letter introducing himself and inviting her to correspond. The next day he was shipped overseas for service in World War II.

During the next year, the two grew to know each other through the mail. Each letter was a seed falling on a fertile heart. A romance was budding.

He requested a photograph, but she refused. She felt that if he really cared, it wouldn't matter what she looked like. When the day finally came for him to return from Europe, they scheduled their first meeting - 7pm at the Grand Central Station in New York.

"You'll recognise me", she wrote, "by the red rose I'll be wearing on my lapel". So at 7pm he was in the station looking for a girl whose heart he loved, but whose face he'd never seen.

I'll let Mr Blanchard tell you what happened:

A young woman was coming toward me, her figure long and slim. Her blonde hair lay back in curls from her delicate ears; her eyes were blue as flowers. Her lips and chin had a gentle firmness, and in her pale green suit she was like springtime come alive.

I started toward her, entirely forgetting to notice that she was not wearing a rose. Almost uncontrollably I made one step close to her, and then I saw Hollis Maynell.

She was standing almost directly behind the girl. A woman well past 40, she had greying hair tucked under a worn hat. She was more than plump, her thick-ankled feet thrust into low-heeled shoes.

The girl in the green suit was walking quickly away. I felt as though I was split in two, so keen was my desire to follow her, and yet so deep was my longing for the woman whose spirit had truly companioned me and upheld my own.

And there she stood. Her pale, plump face was gentle and sensible; her grey eyes had a warm and kindly twinkle. I did not hesitate. My fingers gripped the small, worn blue leather copy of the book that was to identify me to her.

This would not be love, but it would be something precious, something perhaps even better than love; a friendship for which I had been and must ever be grateful. I squared my shoulders and saluted and held out the book to the woman, even though while I spoke, I felt choked by the bitterness of my disappointment.

"I'm Lieutenant John Blanchard, and you must be Miss Maynell. I am so glad you could meet me; may I take you to dinner?" The woman's face broadened into a tolerant smile.

"I don't know what this is about, son," she answered, "but the young lady in the green suit who just went by, she begged me to wear this rose on my coat.

"And she said if you were to ask me out to dinner, I should go and tell you that she is waiting for you in the big restaurant across the street. She said it was some kind of test!"

Author Unknown

THE EMPEROR AND THE SEED

An emperor in the Far East was growing old and knew it was time to choose his successor. Instead of choosing one of his assistants or his children, he decided to do something different. He called the young people in the kingdom together one day. He said, "It is time for me to step down and choose the next emperor. I have decided to choose one of you."

The kids were shocked! But the emperor continued. "I am going to give each one of you a seed today. One very special seed. I want you to plant the seed, water it and come back here one year from today with what you have grown from this one seed. I will then judge the plants that you bring, and the one I choose will be the next emperor!"

137

One boy named Ling was there that day and he, like the others, received a seed. He went home and excitedly told his mother the story. She helped him get a pot and planting soil, and he planted the seed and watered it carefully. Every day he would water it and watch to see if it had grown. After about three weeks, some of the other youths began to talk about their seeds and the plants that were beginning to grow.

Ling kept checking his seed, but nothing ever grew. Three weeks, four weeks, five weeks went by. Still nothing. By now, others were talking about their plants but Ling didn't have a plant, and he felt like a failure. Six months went by - still nothing in Ling's pot. He just knew he had killed his seed.

Everyone else had trees and tall plants, but he had nothing. Ling didn't say anything to his friends, however. He just kept waiting for his seed to grow.

A year finally went by and all the kids of the kingdom brought their plants to the emperor for inspection. Ling told his mother that he wasn't going to take an empty pot. His mother told him to be honest about what had happened. Ling felt sick to his stomach, but he knew his mother was right. He took his empty pot to the palace. When Ling arrived, he was amazed at the variety of plants grown by the other youths. They were beautiful - in all shapes and sizes. Ling put his empty pot on the floor and many of the other kids laughed at him. A few felt sorry for him and just said, "Hey, nice try."

When the emperor arrived, he surveyed the room and greeted the young people. Ling just tried to hide in the back. "My, what great plants, trees and flowers you have grown," said the emperor. "Today, one of you will be appointed the next emperor!" All of a sudden, the emperor spotted Ling at the back of the room with his empty pot. He ordered his guards to bring him to the front. Ling was terrified. "The emperor knows I'm a failure! Maybe he will have me killed!"

When Ling got to the front, the Emperor asked his name. "My name is Ling," he replied. All the kids were laughing and making fun of him. The emperor asked everyone to quieten down. He looked at Ling, and then announced to the crowd, "Behold your new emperor! His name is Ling!" Ling couldn't believe it. Ling couldn't even grow his seed. How could he be the new emperor?

Then the emperor said, "One year ago today, I gave everyone here a seed. I told you to take the seed, plant it, water it and bring it back to me today. But I gave you all boiled seeds which would not grow. All of you, except Ling, have brought me trees and plants and flowers. When you found that the seed would not grow, you substituted another seed for the one I gave you. Ling was the only one with the courage and honesty to bring me a pot with my seed in it. Therefore, he is the one who will be the new emperor!"

Adapted from various versions on the internet.

BREAKING THE SUGAR HABIT

During 1930s, a young boy had become obsessed with eating sugar. His mother was very upset with this. But no matter how much she scolded him and tried to break his habit, he continued to satisfy his sweet tooth. Totally frustrated, she decided to take her son to see his idol – Mahatma Gandhi. Perhaps her son would listen to him.

They walked miles, for hours under a scorching sun to finally reach Gandhi's ashram. There, she shared with Gandhi her predicament.

"Bapu, my son eats too much sugar. It is not good for his health. Would you please advise him to stop eating it?"

Gandhi listened to the woman carefully, thought for a while and replied, "Please come back after two weeks. I will talk to your son."

The woman looked perplexed and wondered why he had not asked the boy to stop eating sugar right away. She took the boy by the hand and went home.

Two weeks later they revisited Gandhi. Gandhi looked directly at the boy and said,

"Boy, you should stop eating sugar. It is not good for your health."

The boy nodded and promised he would not continue this habit any longer. The boy's mother was puzzled. She turned to Gandhi and asked, "Bapu, why didn't you tell him that two weeks ago, when I brought him here to see you?"

Gandhi smiled and said, "Mother, two weeks ago I was eating a lot of sugar myself!"

Attributed to Mahatma Gandhi, adapted from versions on the internet

CHAPTER TWELVE : KINDNESS

THE OLD WOMAN AND THE STRANGER

One day a man saw an old lady stranded on the side of the road, and in the dim light of day he could see she needed help. So he pulled up in front of her Mercedes and got out. His Pinto was still sputtering when he approached her.

Even with the smile on his face, the lady was worried. No one had stopped to help for the last hour or so. Was he going to hurt her? He didn't look safe; he looked poor and hungry.

He could see that she was frightened, standing out there in the cold. He knew how she felt. It was that chill which only fear can put in you. He said, "I'm here to help you, ma'am. Why don't you wait in the car where it's warm? By the way, my name is Bryan Anderson."

Well, all she had was a flat tyre, but for an old lady that was bad enough. Bryan crawled under the car looking for a place to put the jack, skinning his knuckles a couple of times. Soon he was able to change the tyre, but he had to get dirty and his hands hurt. As he was tightening up the lug nuts, she rolled down the window and began to talk to him. She told him that she was from St. Louis and was only just passing through. She couldn't thank him enough for coming to her aid.

Bryan just smiled as he closed her trunk. The lady asked how much she owed him. Any amount would have been all right with her. She already imagined all the awful things that could have happened, had he not stopped.

Bryan never thought twice about being paid. This was not a job to him. This was helping someone in need and God knows, there were plenty who had given him a hand in the past. He had lived his whole life that way, and it never occurred to him to act any other way.

He told her that if she really wanted to pay him back, the next time she saw someone who needed help she could give that person the assistance they needed. Bryan added, "And think of me."

He waited until she started her car and drove off. It had been a cold and depressing day, but he felt good as he headed for home, disappearing into the twilight.

A few miles down the road the lady saw a small café. She went in to grab a bite to eat and take the chill off before she made the last leg of her trip home. It was a dingy looking restaurant. Outside were two old gas pumps. The whole scene was unfamiliar to her. The waitress came over and brought a clean towel to wipe her wet hair.

She had a sweet smile, one that even being on her feet for the whole day couldn't erase. The lady noticed the waitress was nearly eight months pregnant, but she never let the strain and aches change her attitude. The old lady wondered how someone who had so little could be so giving to a stranger.

Then she remembered Bryan.

After the lady finished her meal she paid with a hundred-dollar bill. The waitress quickly went to get change for her but the old lady had slipped right out the door and was gone by the time the waitress came back. The waitress wondered where the lady could be. Then she noticed something written on the napkin.

There were tears in her eyes when she read what the lady wrote: "You don't owe me anything. I have been there too. Somebody once helped me out, the way I'm helping you. If you really want to pay me back, here is what you do: do not let this chain of love end with you."

Under the napkin were four more $100 bills.

Well, there were tables to clear, sugar bowls to fill and people to serve, but the waitress made it through another day. That night when she got home from work and climbed into bed, she was thinking about the money and what the lady had written. How could the lady have known how much she and her husband needed it? With the baby due next month, it was going to be hard.

She knew how worried her husband was. As he lay sleeping next to her, she gave him a soft kiss and whispered soft and low: "Everything's going to be all right. I love you, Bryan Anderson."

Based on a song by country music artist Clay Walker

SOMETHING FOR STEVIE

I try not to be biased, but I had my doubts about hiring Stevie. His placement counsellor assured me that he would be a good, reliable busboy. But I had never had a mentally handicapped employee and wasn't sure I wanted one. I wasn't sure how my customers would react to Stevie.

He was short and a little dumpy, with the smooth facial features and thick-tongued speech of someone with Down's Syndrome. I wasn't worried about most of my trucker customers because truckers don't generally care who buses tables as long as the meatloaf platter is good and the pies are homemade.

The four-wheeler drivers were the ones who concerned me; the mouthy college kids travelling to school; the yuppie snobs who secretly polish their silverware with their napkins for fear of catching some dreaded 'truck stop germ'; the pairs of white-shirted business men on expense accounts who think every truck stop waitress wants to be flirted with.

I knew those people would be uncomfortable around Stevie so I closely watched him for the first few weeks. I shouldn't have worried. After the first week, Stevie had my staff wrapped around his stubby little finger, and within a month my truck regulars had adopted him as their official truck-stop mascot. After that, I really didn't care what the rest of the customers thought of him. He was like a 21-year-old in blue jeans and Nikes, eager to laugh and eager to please, but fierce in his attention to his duties. Every salt and pepper shaker was exactly in its place and not a bread crumb or coffee spill was visible when Stevie got done with the table. Our only problem was convincing him to wait to clean a table until after the customers were finished. He would hover in the background, shifting his weight from one foot to the other, scanning the dining room until a table was empty. Then he would scurry to the empty table, carefully bus the dishes and glasses onto the cart and meticulously wipe the table up with a practiced flourish of his rag. If he thought a customer was watching, his brow would pucker with added concentration. He took pride in doing his job exactly right, and you had to love how hard he tried to please each and every person he met.

Over time, we learned that he lived with his mother, a widow who was disabled after repeated surgeries for cancer. They lived on their Social Security benefits, in public housing, two miles from the truck stop. Their social worker, who stopped to check on him every so often, admitted they had fallen between the cracks. Money was tight, and what I paid him was probably the difference between them being able to live together and Stevie being sent to a group home.

That's why the restaurant was a gloomy place that morning last August, the first morning in three years that Stevie missed work. He was at the Mayo Clinic in Rochester getting a new valve or something put in his heart. His social worker said that people with Down's Syndrome often have heart problems at an early age so this wasn't unexpected, and there was a good chance he would come through the surgery in good shape and be back at work in a few months.

A ripple of excitement ran through the staff later that morning when word came that he was out of surgery, in recovery and doing fine. Frannie, my head waitress, let out a war hoop and did a little dance in the aisle when she heard

145

the good news. Belle Ringer, one of our regular trucker customers, stared at the sight of the 50-year-old grandmother of four doing a victory shimmy beside his table. Frannie blushed, smoothed her apron and shot Belle Ringer a withering look.

He grinned. "OK, Frannie, what was that all about?" he asked. "We just got word that Stevie is out of surgery and going to be okay," she said. "I was wondering where he was. I had a new joke to tell him. What was the surgery about?" Frannie quickly told Belle Ringer and the other two drivers sitting at his booth about Stevie's surgery, then sighed. "Yeah, I'm glad he is going to be OK," she said, "but I don't know how he and his mom are going to handle all the bills. From what I hear, they're barely getting by as it is." Belle Ringer nodded thoughtfully, and Frannie hurried off to wait on the rest of her tables.

Since I hadn't had time to round up a busboy to replace Stevie - and really didn't want to replace him - the girls were bussing their own tables that day until we decided what to do. After the morning rush, Frannie walked into my office. She had a couple of paper napkins in her hand and a funny look on her face.

"What's up?" I asked. "I didn't get that table where Belle Ringer and his friends were sitting cleared off after they left, and Pony Pete and Tony Tipper were sitting there when I got back to clean it off," she said. "This was folded and tucked under a coffee cup."

She handed the napkin to me, and three $20 fell onto my desk when I opened it. On the outside, in big, bold letters was printed "Something For Stevie". "Pony Pete asked me what that was all about," she said, "so I told him about Stevie and his mom and everything, and Pete looked at Tony and Tony looked at Pete, and they ended up giving me this." She handed me another paper napkin that had "Something For Stevie" scrawled on its outside. Two $50 bills were tucked within its folds. Frannie looked at me with wet, shiny eyes, shook her head and said, simply, "Truckers!"

That was three months ago. Today is Thanksgiving, the first day Stevie is supposed to be back to work. His placement worker said he's been counting the days until the doctor said he could work, and it didn't matter at all that it was a holiday. He called ten times in the past week, making sure we knew he was coming, fearful that we had forgotten him or that his job was in jeopardy. I arranged to have his mother bring him to work, met them in the parking lot and invited them both to celebrate his day back.

Stevie was thinner and paler, but couldn't stop grinning as he pushed through the doors and headed for the back room where his apron and bussing cart were waiting.

"Hold up there, Stevie, not so fast," I said. I took him and his mother by their arms. "Work can wait for a minute. To celebrate you coming back, breakfast for you and your mother is on me."

I led them toward a large corner booth at the rear of the room. I could feel and hear the rest of the staff following behind as we marched through the dining room. Glancing over my shoulder, I saw booth after booth of grinning truckers empty and join the procession.

We stopped in front of the big table. Its surface was covered with coffee cups, saucers and dinner plates, all sitting slightly crooked on dozens of folded paper napkins.

"First thing you have to do, Stevie, is clean up this mess," I said. I tried to sound stern. Stevie looked at me, and then at his mother, then pulled out one of the napkins. It had "Something for Stevie" printed on the outside. As he picked it up, two $10 bills fell onto the table. Stevie stared at the money, then at all the napkins peeking from beneath the tableware, each with his name printed or scrawled on it.

I turned to his mother. "There's more than $10,000 in cash and cheques on that table, all from truckers and trucking companies that heard about your problems. Happy Thanksgiving!"

Well, it got really noisy about that time, with everybody hollering and shouting, and there were a few tears, as well. But you know what's funny? While everybody else was busy shaking hands and hugging each other, Stevie, with a big, big smile on his face, was busy clearing all the cups and dishes from the table. Best worker I ever hired!

Adapted from various versions on the internet

RED MARBLES

I was at the corner grocery store buying some potatoes. I noticed a small boy, ragged but clean, hungrily appraising a basket of freshly picked green peas.

I paid for my potatoes but was also drawn to the display of fresh green peas. I am a pushover for creamed peas and new potatoes.

Pondering the peas, I couldn't help overhearing the conversation between Mr. Miller, the store owner, and the ragged boy next to me.

"Hello Barry, how are you today?"

"Hello, Mr. Miller. Fine, thank ya.
Those peas sure look good!"

"They are good, Barry. How's your Ma?"

"Fine. Gittin' stronger alla' time."

"Good. Anything I can help you with?"

"No, Sir... just admiring' them peas."

"Would you like to take some home?" asked Mr. Miller.

"No, Sir. Got nothing' to pay for them with."

"Well, what have you to trade me for some of those peas?"

"All I got's my prize marble here."

"Is that right? Let me see it," said Miller.

"Here 'tis. She's a dandy."

"I can see that. Hmm mmm, only thing is that this one is blue and I sort of go for red. Do you have a red one like this at home?" the store owner asked.

"Not zackley but almost."

"Tell you what. Take this sack of peas home with you and next trip this way let me look at that red marble," Mr. Miller told the boy.

"'Sure will. Thanks Mr. Miller."

Mrs. Miller, who had been standing nearby, came over to help me.

With a smile she said, "There are two other boys like him in our community. All three are in very poor circumstances. Jim just loves to bargain with them for peas, apples, tomatoes, or whatever."

"When they come back with their red marbles – and they always do – he decides he doesn't like red after all and he sends them home with a bag of produce for a green marble or an orange one, when they come on their next trip to the store."

I left the store smiling to myself, impressed with this man. A short time later I moved to Colorado, but I never forgot the story of this man, the boys, and their bartering for marbles.

Years went by, each more rapid than the previous one, until I recently had occasion to visit some old friends in that Idaho community. While I was there learned that Mr. Miller had died and they were having his visitation that evening. Knowing my friends wanted to go, I agreed to accompany them. Upon arrival at the mortuary we got in line to meet the relatives of the deceased and to offer whatever words of comfort we could.

Ahead of us in line were three young men. One was in an army uniform and the other two had smart haircuts, dark suits and white shirts... all were very professional looking. They approached Mrs. Miller, standing composed and smiling by her husband's casket.

Each of the young men hugged her, kissed her on the cheek, spoke briefly with her and moved on to the casket. Her misty light blue eyes followed them as, one by one, each young man stopped briefly and placed his own warm hand over the cold pale hand in the casket. Each left the mortuary awkwardly, wiping his eyes.

Our turn came to meet Mrs. Miller. I told her who I was and reminded her of the story from those many years ago and what she had told me about her husband's bartering for marbles. With her eyes glistening, she took my hand and led me to the casket.

"Those three young men who just left were the boys I told you about. They just told me how they appreciated the things Jim 'traded' them. Now, at last, when Jim could not change his mind about colour or size, they came to pay their debt."

"We've never had a great deal of the wealth of this world," she confided. "But right now, Jim would consider himself the richest man in Idaho."

With loving gentleness, she lifted the lifeless fingers of her deceased husband. Resting underneath were three exquisitely shined, red marbles.

We will not be remembered by our words, but by our kind deeds

Adapted from various versions on the internet.

I'M FLYING!

O nce upon a time there was a little boy who was raised in an orphanage. The little boy had always wished that he could fly like a bird. It was very difficult for him to understand why he could not fly. There were birds at the zoo that were much bigger than he, and they could fly. "Why can't I?" he thought. "Is there something wrong with me?" he wondered.

There was another little boy who was crippled. He had always wished that he could walk and run like other little boys and girls. "Why can't I be like them?" he thought.

One day the little orphan boy, who had wanted to fly like a bird, ran away from the orphanage. He came upon a park where he saw the little boy, who could not walk or run, playing in the sandbox.

He ran over to the little boy and asked him if he had ever wanted to fly like a bird.

"No," said the little boy who could not walk or run. "But I have wondered what it would be like to walk and run like other boys and girls."

"That is very sad," said the little boy who wanted to fly. "Do you think we could be friends?" he said to the little boy in the sandbox.

"Sure," said the little boy.

The two little boys played for hours. They made sand castles and made really funny sounds with their mouths. Sounds which made them laugh really hard. Then the little boy's father came with a wheelchair to pick up his son. The little boy who had always wanted to fly ran over to the boy's father and whispered something into his ear.

"That would be OK," said the man.

The little boy who had always wanted to fly like a bird ran over to his new friend and said, "You are my only friend and I wish that there was something that I could do to make you walk and run like other little boys and girls. But I can't. But there is something that I can do for you."

The little orphan boy turned around and told his new friend to slide up onto his back. He then began to run across the grass. Faster and faster he ran, carrying the little crippled boy on his back. Faster and harder he ran across the park. Harder and harder he made his legs travel. Soon the wind just whistled across the two little boys' faces.

The little boy's father began to cry as he watched his beautiful little crippled son flapping his arms up and down in the wind, all the while yelling at the top of his voice:

"I'M FLYING, DADDY. I'M FLYING!"

By Roger Dean Kiser, Sr.

BOBBY'S GIFT

Bobby was getting cold sitting out in his back yard in the snow. Bobby didn't wear boots; he didn't like them and anyway he didn't own any. The thin sneakers he wore had a few holes in them and they did a poor job of keeping out the cold. Bobby had been in his backyard for about an hour already. And, try as he might, he could not come up with an idea for his mother's Christmas gift. He shook his head as he thought, "This is useless. Even if I do come up with an idea, I don't have any money to spend."

Ever since his father had passed away three years ago, the family of five had struggled. It wasn't because his mother didn't care, or try; there just never seemed to be enough. She worked nights at the hospital, but the small wage that she was earning could only be stretched so far.

What the family lacked in money and material things, they more than made up for in love and family unity. Bobby had two older and one younger sister, who ran the household in their mother's absence. All three of his sisters had already made beautiful gifts for their mother. Somehow it just wasn't fair. Here it was, Christmas Eve already, and he had nothing.

Wiping a tear from his eye, Bobby kicked the snow and started to walk down to the street where the shops and stores were. It wasn't easy being six without a father, especially when he needed a man to talk to.

Bobby walked from shop to shop, looking into each decorated window. Everything seemed so beautiful and so out of reach. It was starting to get dark and Bobby reluctantly turned to walk home when suddenly his eyes caught the glimmer of the setting sun's rays reflecting off something along the curb. He reached down and discovered a shiny dime.

Never before has anyone felt as wealthy as Bobby felt at that moment. As he held his new-found treasure, warmth spread throughout his entire body and he walked into the first store he saw. His excitement quickly turned cold when salesperson after salesperson told him that he could not buy anything with only a dime.

He saw a flower shop and went inside to wait in line. When the shop owner asked if he could help him, Bobby presented the dime and asked if he could buy one flower for his mother's Christmas gift. The shop owner looked at Bobby and his ten-cent offering. Then he put his hand on Bobby's shoulder and said to him, "You just wait here and I'll see what I can do for you."

As Bobby waited, he looked at the beautiful flowers and even though he was a boy, he could see why mothers and girls liked flowers. The sound of the door closing as the last customer left jolted Bobby back to reality. All alone in the shop, Bobby began to feel afraid.

Suddenly the shop owner came out and moved to the counter. There, before Bobby's eyes, lay twelve long-stem, red roses, with leaves of green and tiny white flowers all tied together with a big silver bow. Bobby's heart sank as the owner picked them up and placed them gently into a long white box.

"That will be ten cents young man," the shop owner said, reaching out his hand for the dime. Slowly, Bobby moved his hand to give the man his dime. Could this be true? No one else would give him a thing for his dime! Sensing the boy's reluctance, the shop owner added, "I just happened to have some roses on sale for ten cents a dozen. Would you like them?"

This time Bobby did not hesitate, and when the man placed the long box into his hands, he knew it was true. Walking out the door that the owner was holding for Bobby, he heard the shop keeper say, "Merry Christmas, son."

As he returned inside, the shop keeper's wife walked out. "Who were you talking to back there and where are the roses you were fixing?" Staring out the window and blinking back the tears from his eyes, he replied: "A strange thing happened to me this morning. While I was setting up things to open the shop, I thought I heard a voice telling me to set aside a dozen of my best roses for a special gift. I wasn't sure at the time whether I had lost my mind or what, but I set them aside anyway. Then just a few minutes ago, a little boy came into the shop and wanted to buy a flower for his mother with one small dime.

"When I looked at him, I saw myself, many years ago. I too was a poor boy with no money to buy my mother a Christmas gift. A bearded man, whom I never knew, stopped me on the street and told me that he wanted to give me ten dollars.

"When I saw that little boy tonight, I knew who that voice was, and I put together a dozen of my very best roses."

The shop owner and his wife hugged each other tightly, and as they stepped out into the bitter cold air, they somehow didn't feel cold at all.

Adapted from various versions on the internet

THE IMPORTANCE OF
TAKING RISKS SOMETIMES

A number of years ago, I had the opportunity to play the character of Ronald McDonald for the McDonald's Corporation. My marketplace covered most of Arizona and a portion of Southern California.

One of our standard events was "Ronald Day." One day each month, we visited as many of the community hospitals as possible, bringing a little happiness into a place where no one ever looks forward to going.

I was very proud to be able to make a difference for children and adults who were experiencing some 'down time.' The warmth and gratification I would receive stayed with me for weeks. I loved the project, McDonald's loved the project, the kids and adults loved it and so did the nursing and hospital staff.

There were two restrictions placed on me during a visit. First, I could not go anywhere in the hospital without McDonald's personnel (my handlers) and the hospital personnel. That way, if I were to walk into a room and frighten a child, there was someone there to address the issue immediately. And second, I could not physically touch anyone within the hospital. They did not want me transferring germs from one patient to another. I understood why they had this 'don't touch' rule, but I didn't like it. I believe that touching is the most honest form of communication we will ever know. Printed and spoken words can lie; it is impossible to lie with a warm hug.

Breaking either of these rules, I was told, meant I could lose my job. Towards the end of my fourth year of "Ronald Days," as I was heading down a hallway on my way home after a long day in grease paint and I heard a little voice calling, "Ronald, Ronald!"

I stopped. The soft little voice was coming through a half-opened door. I pushed the door open and saw a young boy, about five years old, lying in his dad's arms, hooked up to more medical equipment than I had ever seen. Mom was on the other side, along with Grandma, Grandpa and a nurse tending to the equipment.

I knew by the feeling in the room that the situation was grave. I asked the little boy his name - he told me it was Billy - and I did a few simple magic tricks for him. As I stepped back to say good-bye, I asked Billy if there was anything else I could do for him.

"Ronald, would you hold me?" Such a simple request. But what ran through my mind was that if I touched him, I could lose my job. So, I told Billy I could not do that right now, but I suggested that he and I colour a picture. Upon completing a wonderful piece of art that we were both very proud of, Billy asked me to hold him again. By this time my heart was screaming "Yes!" But my mind was screaming louder; "No, you are going to lose your job!"

This second time that Billy asked me, I had to ponder why I could not grant the simple request of a little boy who would probably not be going home. I asked myself why was I being logically and emotionally torn apart by someone I had never seen before and would probably never see again.

"Hold me." It was such a simple request, and yet... I searched for any reasonable response that would allow me to leave. I could not come up with a single one. It took me a moment to realise that in this situation, losing my job may not be the disaster I feared. Was losing my job the worst thing in the world?

Did I have enough self-belief that if I did lose my job, I would be able to pick up and start again? The answer was a loud, bold, affirming "Yes!". I could pick up and start again. So what was the risk?

Just that if I lost my job, it probably would not be long before I would first lose my car, then my home... and to be honest with you, I really liked those things. But I realised that at the end of my life, the car would have no value and neither would the house. The only things that had steadfast value were experiences.

Once I reminded myself that the real reason I was there was to bring a little happiness to an unhappy environment, I realised that I really faced no risk at all. I sent Mom, Dad, Grandma and Grandpa out of the room, and my two McDonald's escorts out to the van. The nurse tending the medical equipment stayed, but Billy asked her to stand and face the corner. Then I picked up this little wonder of a human being.

He was so frail and so scared. We laughed and cried for 45 minutes, and talked about the things that worried him. Billy was afraid that his little brother might get lost coming home from kindergarten next year, without Billy to show him the way. He worried that his dog wouldn't get another bone because Billy had hidden the bones in the house before going back to the hospital, and now he couldn't remember where he put them. These are problems to a little boy who knows he is not going home.

On my way out of the room, with tear-streaked makeup running down my neck, I gave Mom and Dad my real name and phone number (another automatic dismissal from McDonald's, but I figured that I was gone and had nothing to lose), and said if there was anything the McDonald's Corporation or I could do, to give me a call and consider it done.

Less than 48 hours later, I received a phone call from Billy's mom. She informed me that Billy had passed away. She and her husband simply wanted to thank me for making a difference in their little boy's life.

Billy's mom told me that shortly after I left the room, Billy looked at her and said, "Momma, I don't care anymore if I see Santa this year because...I was held by Ronald McDonald!"

Sometimes we must do what is right for the moment, regardless of the perceived risk. Only experiences have value, and the one biggest reason people limit their experiences is because of the risk involved.

For the record, McDonald's did find out about Billy and me, but, given the circumstances, permitted me to retain my job. I continued as Ronald for another year before leaving the corporation to share the story of Billy and how important it is to take risks.

By Jeff McMullen

THE CAB RIDE I'LL NEVER FORGET

Twenty years ago, I drove a cab for a living. One night I took a fare at 2:30 am, and when I arrived to collect, the building was dark except for a single light in a ground floor window. Under these circumstances, many drivers would just honk once.

But I had seen too many impoverished people who depended on taxis as their only means of transportation. Unless a situation smelled of danger, I always went to the door. This passenger might be someone who needs my assistance, I reasoned to myself. So I walked to the door and knocked.

"Just a minute," answered a frail, elderly voice. I could hear something being dragged across the floor. After a long pause, the door opened. A small woman in her eighties stood before me. She was wearing a print dress and a pillbox hat with a veil pinned on it, like somebody out of a 1940s movie. By her side was a small nylon suitcase.

The apartment looked as if no one had lived in it for years. All the furniture was covered with sheets. There were no clocks on the walls, no knickknacks or utensils on the counters. In the corner was a cardboard box filled with photos and glassware.

'Would you carry my bag out to the car?' she said. I took the suitcase to the cab, and then returned to assist the woman. She took my arm and we walked slowly toward the curb.

She kept thanking me for my kindness. "It's nothing," I told her. "I just try to treat my passengers the way I would want my mother to be treated."

"Oh, you're such a good boy," she said.

When we got in the cab, she gave me an address and then asked, "Could you drive through downtown?"

"It's not the shortest way," I answered quickly.

"Oh, I don't mind," she said "I'm in no hurry. I'm on my way to a hospice."

I looked in the rear-view mirror. Her eyes were glistening. "I don't have any family left," she continued. "The doctor says I don't have very long."

I quietly reached over and shut off the meter. "What route would you like me to take?" I asked. For the next two hours, we drove through the city. She showed me the building where she had once worked as an elevator operator. We drove through the neighbourhood where she and her husband had lived when they were newlyweds. She had me pull up in front of a furniture warehouse that had once been a ballroom where she had gone dancing as a girl.

Sometimes she'd ask me to slow in front of a particular building or corner and would sit staring into the darkness, saying nothing.

As the first hint of sun was creasing the horizon, she suddenly said, "I'm tired. Let's go now." We drove in silence to the address she had given me. It was a low building, like a small convalescent home, with a driveway that passed under a portico.

Two orderlies came out to the cab as soon as we pulled up. They were solicitous and intent, watching her every move. They must have been expecting her. I opened the trunk and took the small suitcase to the door. The woman was already seated in a wheelchair. "How much do I owe you?" she asked, reaching into her purse.

"Nothing," I said.

"You have to make a living," she answered.

"There are other passengers," I responded.

Almost without thinking, I bent and gave her a hug. She held onto me tightly. "You gave an old woman a little moment of joy," she said. "Thank you." I squeezed her hand, and then walked into the dim morning light. Behind me, a door shut. It was the sound of the closing of a life.

I didn't pick up any more passengers that shift. I drove aimlessly, lost in thought. For the rest of that day, I could hardly talk.

What if that woman had got an angry driver, or one who was impatient to end his shift? What if I had refused to take the run, or had honked once, then driven away? On a quick review, I don't think that I have done anything more important in my life.

We're conditioned to think that our lives revolve around great moments. But great moments often catch us unaware - beautifully wrapped in what others may consider a small one.

People may not remember exactly what you did or what you said, but they will always remember how you made them feel.

By Kent Nerburn

CHAPTER THIRTEEN : LESSONS LEARNED

THE GARBAGE TRUCK

One day, I hopped into a taxi and took off for the airport. We were driving in the right lane when suddenly, a black car jumped out of a parking space right in front of us. My taxi driver slammed the brakes, skidded, and missed the other car by just a few inches! The driver of the other car whipped his head around and started yelling at us. My taxi driver just smiled and waved at the guy. I mean, he was really friendly.

So I asked, "Why did you just do that? This guy almost ruined your car and sent us to the hospital!" This is when my taxi driver taught me what I now call 'The Law of the Garbage Truck'.

He explained, "Many people are like garbage trucks. They run around full of garbage, full of frustration, full of anger, and full of disappointment. As their garbage piles up, they need a place to dump it and sometimes they'll dump it on you. Never take it personally. Just smile, wave, wish them well and move on with life. Don't take their garbage and spread it onto other people at work, at home or on the streets."

Adapted from various versions on the internet

THE FENCE

There once was a little boy who had a bad temper. His father gave him a bag of nails and told him that every time he lost his temper, he must hammer a nail into the back of the fence. The first day the boy had driven thirty-seven nails into the fence. Over the next few weeks, as he learned to control his anger, the number of nails hammered daily gradually dwindled down. He discovered it was easier to hold his temper than to drive those nails into the fence.

Finally, the day came when the boy didn't lose his temper at all. He told his father about it and the father suggested that the boy now pull out one nail for each day that he was able to hold his temper. The days passed and the young boy was finally able to tell his father that all the nails were gone.

The father took his son by the hand and led him to the fence. He said, "You have done well, my son, but look at the holes in the fence. The fence will never be the same. When you say things in anger, they leave a scar just like this one. You can put a knife in a man and draw it out. It won't matter how many times you say I'm sorry, the wound is still there."

Adapted from various versions on the internet

THE GIFT

One day, the Buddha and a large following of monks and nuns were passing through a village. The Buddha chose a large, shaded tree to sit beneath so the group could rest awhile out of the heat. He often chose times like these to teach, and so he began to speak. Soon, villagers heard about the visiting teacher and many gathered around to hear him.

One surly young man stood to the side, watching, as the crowd grew larger and larger. To him, it seemed that there were too many people traveling from the city to his village, and each had something to sell or teach. Impatient with the bulging crowd of monks and villagers, he shouted at the Buddha, "Go away! You just want to take advantage of us! You teachers come here to say a few pretty words and then ask for food and money!" But the Buddha was unruffled by these insults. He remained calm, exuding a feeling of loving kindness. He politely requested that the man come forward. Then he asked, "Young sir, if you purchased a lovely gift for someone, but that person did not accept the gift, to whom does the gift then belong?"

The odd question took the young man by surprise. "I guess the gift would still be mine because I was the one who bought it."

"Exactly so," replied the Buddha. "Now, you have just cursed me and been angry with me. But if I do not accept your curses, if I do not get insulted and angry in return, these curses will fall back upon you—the same as the gift returning to its owner."

The young man clasped his hands together and slowly bowed to the Buddha. It was an acknowledgement that a valuable lesson had been learned. And so the Buddha concluded for all to hear: "As a mirror reflects an object, as a still lake reflects the sky; take care that what you speak or act is for good. For goodness will always cast back goodness and harm will always cast back harm."

Adapted from various versions on the internet

TEN GOOD REASONS WE ALL NEED TO HUG EACH DAY

Hugging therapy is definitely a powerful way of healing. Research shows that hugging (and also laughter) is extremely effective at healing sickness, disease, loneliness, depression, anxiety and stress.

Research shows a proper deep hug, where the hearts are pressing together, can benefit you in these ways:

1. The nurturing touch of a hug builds trust and a sense of safety. This helps with open and honest communication.

2. Hugs can instantly boost oxytocin levels, which heal feelings of loneliness, isolation and anger.

3. Holding a hug for an extended time lifts one's serotonin levels, elevating mood and creating happiness.

4. Hugs strengthen the immune system. The gentle pressure on the sternum and the emotional charge this

creates activates the Solar Plexus Chakra. This stimulates the thymus gland, which regulates and balances the body's production of white blood cells, which keep you healthy and disease-free.

5. Hugging boosts self-esteem. From the time we're born our family's touch shows us that we're loved and special. The associations of self-worth and tactile sensations from our early years are still imbedded in our nervous system as adults. The cuddles we received from our Mum and Dad while growing up remain imprinted at a cellular level, and hugs remind us of that at a somatic level. Hugs, therefore, connect us to our ability to self-love.

6. Hugging relaxes muscles. Hugs release tension in the body. Hugs can take away pain; they soothe aches by increasing circulation into the soft tissues.

7. Hugs balance out the nervous system. The galvanic skin response of someone receiving and giving a hug shows a change in skin conductance. The effect in moisture and electricity in the skin suggests a more balanced state in the parasympathetic nervous system.

8. Hugs teach us how to give and receive. There is equal value in receiving and being receptive to warmth, as to giving and sharing. Hugs educate us about how love flows both ways.

9. Hugs are so much like meditation and laughter. They teach us to let go and be present in the moment. They encourage us to flow with the energy of life. Hugs get you out of your circular thinking patterns and connect you with your heart, your feelings and your breath.

10. The energy exchange between the people hugging is an investment in the relationship. It encourages empathy and understanding.

Adapted from various sources on the internet

■ ■ ■

AS I BEGAN TO LOVE MYSELF

1.   As I began to love myself, I found that anguish and emotional suffering were only warning signs that I was living against my own truth. Today, I know this is "AUTHENTICITY".

2.   As I began to love myself I understood how much it can offend somebody if I try to force my desires on this person - even though I knew the time was not right and the person was not ready for it, and even though this person was me. Today I call it "RESPECT".

3.   As I began to love myself I stopped craving a different life, and I could see that everything that surrounded me was inviting me to grow. Today I call it "MATURITY".

4.   As I began to love myself I understood that in any circumstance, I am in the right place at the right time, and everything happens at the exact right moment. So I could be calm. Today I call it "SELF-CONFIDENCE".

5.   As I began to love myself I quit stealing my own time, and I stopped designing huge projects for the future. Today, I only do what brings me joy and happiness, things I love to do and that make my heart cheer, and I do them in my own way and in my own rhythm. Today I call it "SIMPLICITY".

169

6.   As I began to love myself I freed myself from anything that is no good for my health; food, people, things, situations and everything that drew me down and away from myself. At first I called this attitude a healthy egoism. Today I know it is "LOVE OF ONESELF".

7.   As I began to love myself I quit trying to always be right, and ever since, I have been wrong less of the time. Today I discovered that is "MODESTY".

8.   As I began to love myself I refused to go on living in the past and worrying about the future. Now, I only live for the moment, where everything is happening. Today I live each day, and day by day, and I call it "FULFILLMENT".

9.   As I began to love myself I recognised that my mind can disturb me and it can make me sick. But as I connected it to my heart, my mind became a valuable ally. Today I call this connection "WISDOM OF THE HEART".

10. We no longer need to fear arguments, confrontations or any kind of problems with ourselves or others. Even stars collide, and out of their crashing, new worlds are born. Today I know "THAT IS LIFE".

By Charlie Chaplin (1889-1977), English comic actor, filmmaker and composer.

THE STORY OF TEDDY STODDARD

As she stood in front of her fifth-grade class on the very first day of school, she told the children an untruth. Like most teachers, she looked at her students and said that she loved them all the same. However, that was impossible, because there in the front row, slumped in his seat, was a little boy named Teddy Stoddard.

Mrs. Thompson had watched Teddy the year before and noticed that he did not play well with the other children, that his clothes were messy and that he constantly needed a bath. In addition, Teddy could be unpleasant. It got to the point where Mrs. Thompson would actually take delight in marking his papers with a broad red pen, making bold Xs and then putting a big 'F' at the top of his papers.

At the school where Mrs. Thompson taught, she was required to review each child's past records and she put Teddy's off until last. However, when she reviewed his file, she was in for a surprise.

Teddy's first-grade teacher wrote, 'Teddy is a bright child with a ready laugh. He does his work neatly and has good manners... he is a joy to be around.'

His second-grade teacher wrote, 'Teddy is an excellent student, well-liked by his classmates, but he is troubled because his mother has a terminal illness and life at home must be a struggle.'

His third-grade teacher wrote, 'His mother's death has been hard on him. He tries to do his best, but his father doesn't show much interest, and his home life will soon affect him if some steps aren't taken.'

Teddy's fourth-grade teacher wrote, 'Teddy is withdrawn and doesn't show much interest in school. He doesn't have many friends and he sometimes sleeps in class.'

By now, Mrs. Thompson realised the problem and she was ashamed of herself. She felt even worse when her students brought her Christmas presents, wrapped in beautiful ribbons and bright paper, except for Teddy's. His present was clumsily wrapped in the heavy, brown paper that was a re-used grocery bag.

Mrs. Thompson took pains to open it in the middle of the other presents. Some of the children started to laugh when she found a rhinestone bracelet with some of the stones missing, and a bottle that was one-quarter full of perfume. But she stifled the children's laughter when she exclaimed how pretty the bracelet was, putting it on, and dabbing some of the perfume on her wrist. Teddy Stoddard stayed after school that day just long enough to say, "Mrs. Thompson, today you smelled just like my Mom used to."

After the children left, she cried for at least an hour. On that very day, she quit teaching reading, writing and arithmetic. Instead, she began to teach children.... Mrs. Thompson paid particular attention to Teddy. As she worked with him, his mind seemed to come alive. The more she encouraged him, the faster he responded.

By the end of the year, Teddy had become one of the smartest children in the class and, despite her lie that she would love all the children the same, Teddy became one of her 'teacher's pets'.

A year later, she found a note under her door, from Teddy, telling her that she was the best teacher he'd ever had in his whole life.

Six years went by before she got another note from Teddy. He then wrote that he had finished high school, third in his class, and she was still the best teacher he ever had in life.

Four years after that, she got another letter, saying that while things had been tough at times, he'd stayed in school, had stuck with it, and would soon graduate from college with the highest of honours. He assured Mrs. Thompson that she was still the best and favourite teacher he had ever had in his whole life.

Four more years passed and yet another letter came. This time he explained that after he got his bachelor's degree, he decided to go a little further. The letter explained that she was still the best and favourite teacher he'd ever had.

But now his name was a little longer.... The letter was signed, Theodore F. Stoddard, MD.

The story does not end there.

You see, there was yet another letter that spring. Teddy said he had met this girl and was going to be married. He explained that his father had died a couple of years ago and he was wondering if Mrs. Thompson might agree to sit at the wedding in the place that was usually reserved for the mother of the groom. Of course, Mrs. Thompson did.

And guess what? She wore that bracelet, the one with several rhinestones missing. Moreover, she made sure she was wearing the perfume that Teddy remembered his mother wearing on their last Christmas together.

They hugged each other, and Dr Stoddard whispered in Mrs. Thompson's ear, "Thank you, Mrs. Thompson, for believing in me. Thank you so much for making me feel important and showing me that I could make a difference."

Mrs. Thompson, with tears in her eyes, whispered back, "Teddy, you have it all wrong. You were the one who taught me that I could make a difference. I didn't know how to teach until I met you."

As told by Dr Wayne Dyer. Teddy Stoddard is a doctor at the Stoddard Cancer Centre in Des Moines, Iowa.

CHAPTER FOURTEEN : LIVING IN THE NOW

HUMANITY

Question: "What thing about humanity surprises you the most?"

Answer: "Man...because he sacrifices his health in order to make money.

Then he sacrifices money to recuperate his health.

And then he is so anxious about the future that he does not enjoy the present.

The result being that he does not live in the present or the future.

He lives as if he is never going to die, and then dies having never really lived."

The Dalai Lama

Adapted from various versions on the internet

■ ■ ■

SLOW DANCE

Have you ever watched kids on a merry-go-round?
Or listened to rain slapping the ground?

175

Ever followed a butterfly's erratic flight,
Or gazed at the sun fading into the night?

You better slow down, don't dance so fast,
Time is short, the music won't last.

Do you run through each day on the fly?
When you ask "How are you?", do you hear the reply?

When the day is done, do you lie in your bed?
With the next hundred chores running through your head?

You better slow down, don't dance so fast,
Time is short, the music won't last.

Ever told your child, we'll do it tomorrow,
And in your haste, not see his sorrow?

Ever lost touch, let a friendship die,
Cause you never had time to call and say 'hi'?

You better slow down, don't dance so fast,
Time is short, the music won't last.

When you run so fast to get somewhere,
You miss half the fun of getting there.

When you worry and hurry through your day,
It's like an unopened gift thrown away.

Life isn't a race, so take it slower,
Hear the music before your song is over.

By David L Weatherford

EMPTY PAGES

One evening a young woman went out alone to walk barefoot by the ocean after the sun had set. She stopped in her path and turned so she could see the footsteps she had left in the sand. But they had already been washed away by the waves. When she turned to continue her walk, she was startled by the presence of an old woman who appeared out of nowhere, wrapped in a blanket and sitting by a fire, slowly paging through the leaves of a leather-covered book.

She walked up to the woman and asked, "Where did you come from? I didn't see you here a moment ago. And how did you start this fire so quickly?"

Her questions went unanswered but were instead met with a reply in a serene voice, "Sit with me, child. I have something to show you."

As the young woman sat down beside the fire, the mysterious stranger handed her the book. She curiously turned the pages one by one and was amazed to discover they contained the story of her whole life, from the early days of childhood to the present. She then came to the page telling of her encounter with the old woman by the fire during her walk on the beach - but upon turning to the next page, she found it empty.

She frantically began to turn the rest of the pages in the book only to find that they too were all empty. In bewilderment, she looked at the old woman and pleaded with her to explain.

"Does this mean my life ends this night?"

"No, my child. It means tonight your life begins."

At that moment the old woman took the book into her own hands and began to tear out each of the pages, throwing them one by one into the fire until all that was left were blank pages.

She handed the book of empty pages to the young woman.

"You see," she said, "just as the waves washed away your footsteps in the sand, your past is forever gone, never to return. The only moment you ever truly possess is here and now.

"Each new moment is the beginning of the rest of your life and is to be lived to the fullest, for you will not have a chance to live that moment a second time.

"Most important of all, each new day brings an opportunity to love - one that may never come to you again.

"As for your future, you are free to shape it as you wish, for it has not yet been written."

Then, as mysteriously as she had appeared, the old woman stood to walk away and disappeared into the darkness of the night.

By William Oak

■ ■ ■

A STORY TO LIVE BY

My brother-in-law opened the bottom drawer of my sister's bureau and lifted out a tissue-wrapped package. "This," he said, "is not a slip. This is lingerie." He discarded the tissue and handed me the slip. It was exquisite; silk, handmade and trimmed with a cobweb of lace. The price tag, with an astronomical figure on it, was still attached.

"Jan bought this the first time we went to New York, at least eight or nine years ago. She never wore it. She was saving it for a special occasion. Well, I guess this is the occasion." He took the slip from me and put it on the bed with the other clothes we were taking to the mortician. His hands lingered on the soft material for a moment, then he slammed the drawer shut and turned to me. "Don't ever save anything for a special occasion. Every day you're alive is a special occasion."

I remembered those words through the funeral and the days that followed when I helped him and my niece attend to all the sad chores that follow an unexpected death. I thought about them on the plane returning to California from the Midwestern town where my sister's family lives. I thought about all the things that she hadn't seen or heard or done. I thought about the things that she had done without realizing that they were special.

I'm still thinking about his words, and they've changed my life. I'm reading more and dusting less. I'm sitting on the deck and admiring the view without fussing about the weeds in the garden. I'm spending more time with my family and friends, and less time in committee meetings. Whenever possible, life should be a pattern of experience to

179

savour, not endure. I'm trying to recognise these moments now and cherish them.

I'm not "saving" anything; we use our good china and crystal for every 'special event'; losing a pound, getting the sink unstopped, the first camellia blossom.

I wear my good blazer to the market if I feel like it. My theory is, if I look prosperous, I can shell out $28.49 for one small bag of groceries without wincing. I'm not saving my good perfume for special parties; clerks in hardware stores and tellers in banks have noses that function as well as my party-going friends.

"Someday" and "one of these days" are losing their grip on my vocabulary. If it's worth seeing or hearing or doing, I want to see and hear and do it now. I'm not sure what my sister would have done had she known that she wouldn't be here for the tomorrow we all take for granted. I think she would have called family members and a few close friends. She might have called a few former friends to apologise and mend fences for past squabbles. I like to think she would have gone out for a Chinese dinner, her favourite food. I'm guessing - I'll never know.

It's those little things left undone that would make me angry if I knew that my hours were limited. Angry because I put off seeing good friends whom I was going to get in touch with - someday. Angry because I hadn't written certain letters that I intended to write - one of these days. Angry and sorry that I didn't tell my husband and daughter often enough how much I truly love them. I'm trying very hard not to put off, hold back, or save anything that would add laughter and lustre to our lives.

And every morning when I open my eyes, I tell myself that it is special.

Every day, every minute, every breath truly is...a gift from God.

By Ann Wells (Los Angeles Times)

———————— ▪ ▪ ▪ ————————

TAKE TIME

Take time to think - It's the source of all power

Take time to read - It's the foundation of all wisdom

Take time to play - It's the source of perpetual youth

Take time to be quiet - It's the opportunity to listen

Take time to be aware - It's the opportunity to help others

Take time to love and be loved - It's God's greatest gift

Take time to laugh - It's the music of the soul

Take time to be friendly - It's the road to happiness

Take time to dream - It's what the future is made of

Take time to pray - It's the greatest power on earth

Take time to give - It's too short a day to be selfish

Take time to work - It's the price of success.

Author Unknown

DUST IF YOU MUST

"**A** house becomes a home when you can write 'I love you' on the furniture."

I used to spend at least eight hours every weekend making sure things were just perfect "in case someone came over". Finally, I realised one day that no-one came over; they were all out living life and having fun!

NOW, when people visit, I don't have to explain the 'condition' of my home. They are more interested in hearing about the things I've been doing while I was away living life and having fun.

If you haven't figured this out yet, please heed this advice.

Life is short. Enjoy it!

Dust if you must... but wouldn't it be better to paint a picture or write a letter, bake cookies or a cake - and lick the spoon? Or plant a seed or ponder the difference between want and need?!

Dust if you must, but there's not much time...with rivers to swim and mountains to climb, music to hear and books to read, friends to cherish and life to lead.

Dust if you must, but the world's out there with the sun in your eyes, the wind in your hair, a flutter of snow and a shower of rain. This day will not come around again.

Dust if you must, but bear in mind, old age will come and it's not kind...

And when you go - and go you must - you, yourself will make more dust!

It's not what you gather, but what you scatter that tells what kind of life you have lived... and remember, a layer of dust protects the wood beneath it!

Author unknown

◼ ◼ ◼

MEDITATION

Buddha was asked,

"What have you gained from meditation?"

He replied, "Nothing!

However, let me tell you what I have lost:

Anger, anxiety, depression, insecurity, fear of old age and death."

Adapted from sources on the internet

CHAPTER FIFTEEN :
LOVE

NO MATTER WHAT, WHERE OR WHEN

I was watching some little children play football. These children were only five or six years old. They were playing a real game - a serious game. There were two teams, complete with coaches, uniforms and parents. I didn't know any of them, so I was able to enjoy the game without the distraction of being anxious about winning or losing. I wished the parents and coaches could have done the same.

The teams were pretty evenly matched. I will just call them Team 1 and Team 2. Nobody scored in the first half. In the second half, the Team 1 coach pulled out his best player and let him go in goal. The game took a dramatic turn.

The Team 2 players swarmed around the little guy. He was an outstanding athlete, but he was no match for the opposition players, who were very good.

Team 2 began to score. The Team 1 goalie gave it everything he had, recklessly throwing his body in front of incoming balls, trying valiantly to stop them. Team 2 scored two goals in quick succession. It infuriated the young boy. He became a raging maniac - shouting, running, diving.

On the next attack, with all the stamina he could muster, he covered the boy who now had the ball. But that boy kicked it to another boy twenty feet away, and by the time the goalie repositioned himself, it was too late - Team 2 scored a third goal.

I soon learned who the goalie's parents were. They were nice, neat-looking people. I could tell that his father had just come from the office - he still had his suit and tie on. They yelled encouragement to their son. I became totally absorbed, watching the boy on the field and his parents on the side-lines. After the third goal, the little boy changed. He could see it was no use, he couldn't stop them. Although he didn't quit, futility was written all over him.

His father changed, too. The man had been urging his son to try harder, yelling advice and encouragement. But then he changed. He became anxious. He tried to say it was okay - to hang in there. He grieved for the pain his son was feeling.

After the fourth goal, I knew what was going to happen. I've seen it before. The little boy needed help so badly, and there was no help to be had. He retrieved the ball from the net and handed it to the referee and then he cried. He just stood there while huge tears rolled down both cheeks. He went to his knees and put his fists to his eyes - and he cried the tears of the helpless and broken-hearted.

When the boy went to his knees, I saw the father panic. His wife clutched his arm and said, "Jim, don't. You'll embarrass him." But he tore loose from her and ran onto the field. He wasn't supposed to - the game was still in progress.

Suit, tie, shirt, shoes and all, he charged onto the field, and he picked up his son so everybody would know that this was his boy, and he hugged him and held him and cried with him.

I've never been so proud of a man in my life. He carried him off the field and when he got close to the side-lines, I heard him say, "Scotty, I'm so proud of you. You were great out there. I want everybody to know that you are my son."

"Daddy," the boy sobbed, "I couldn't stop them. I tried, Daddy, I tried and tried, and they scored on me."

"Scotty, it doesn't matter how many times they scored on you. You're my son, I'm proud of you. I want you to go back out there and finish the game. I know you want to quit, but you can't," he said. "And son, you're going to get scored on again, but it doesn't matter. Go on now."

It made a difference. When you're all alone and you're getting scored on - and you can't stop them - it means a lot to know that it doesn't matter to those who love you.

The little guy ran back on to the field - and the other team scored two more times. But it was okay.

Author Unknown

A SANDPIPER TO BRING YOU JOY!

She was six years old when I first met her on the beach near where I live. I drive to this beach, a distance of three or four miles, whenever the world begins to close in on me. She was building a sand castle or something and looked up, her eyes as blue as the sea.

"Hello," she said. I answered with a nod, not really in the mood to bother with a small child. "I'm building," she said.

"I see that. What is it?" I asked, not really caring.

"Oh, I don't know, I just like the feel of sand."

That sounds good, I thought, and slipped off my shoes. A sandpiper glided by.

"That's a joy," the child said.

"It's a what?" I asked.

"It's a joy, my mama says sandpipers come to bring us joy." The bird went gliding down the beach.

"Goodbye, joy," I muttered to myself, "hello pain," and turned to walk on. I was depressed; my life seemed completely out of balance.

"What's your name?" She wouldn't give up.

"Robert," I answered. "I'm Robert Peterson."

"Mine's Wendy....I'm six."

"Hi, Wendy."

She giggled, "You're funny," she said. In spite of my gloom, I laughed too and walked on. Her musical giggle followed me. "Come again, Mr. P," she called. "We'll have another happy day!"

The days and weeks that followed belonged to others; a group of unruly Boy Scouts, PTA meetings and an ailing mother.

The sun was shining one morning as I took my hands out of the dishwater. "I need a sandpiper," I said to myself, gathering up my coat. The ever-changing balm of the seashore awaited me. The breeze was chilly, but I strode along, trying to recapture the serenity I needed. I had forgotten the child and was startled when she appeared.

"Hello, Mr. P," she said. "Do you want to play?"

"What did you have in mind?" I asked, with a twinge of annoyance.

"I don't know, you say."

"How about charades?" I asked, sarcastically.

Her tinkling laughter burst forth again. "I don't know what that is".

"Then let's just walk," I said. Looking at her, I noticed the delicate fairness of her face. "Where do you live?" I asked.

"Over there." She pointed toward a row of summer cottages. Strange, I thought, in winter.

"Where do you go to school?"

"I don't go to school. Mommy says we're on vacation." She chattered little girl talk as we strolled up the beach, but my mind was on other things. When I left for home, Wendy said it had been a happy day. Feeling surprisingly better, I smiled at her and agreed.

Three weeks later, I rushed to the beach in a state of near panic. I was in no mood to even greet Wendy. I thought I saw her mother on the porch and felt like demanding she keep her child at home. "Look, if you don't mind," I said crossly, when Wendy caught up with me, "I'd rather be alone today." She seemed unusually pale and out of breath.

"Why?" she asked.

I turned to her and shouted, "Because my mother died!" and thought, 'My God, why was I saying this to a little child?'

"Oh," she said quietly, "then this is a bad day."

"Yes," I said, "and yesterday and the day before and - oh, go away!"

"Did it hurt?" she enquired.

"Did what hurt?" I was exasperated with her, with myself.

"When she died?" she asked.

"Of course it hurt!" I snapped, misunderstanding, wrapped up in myself. I strode off.

A month or so after that, when I next went to the beach, she wasn't there. Feeling guilty, ashamed and admitting to myself I missed her, I went up to the cottage after my walk and knocked at the door. A drawn looking young woman with honey-coloured hair opened the door.

"Hello," I said. "I'm Robert Peterson. I missed your little girl today and wondered where she was."

"Oh, yes, Mr. Peterson, please come in. Wendy spoke of you so much. I'm afraid I allowed her to bother you. If she was a nuisance, please, accept my apologies."

"Not at all - she's a delightful child," I said, suddenly realizing that I meant what I had just said.

"Wendy died last week, Mr. Peterson. She had leukaemia. Maybe she didn't tell you."

Struck dumb, I groped for a chair. I had to catch my breath.

"She loved this beach so when she asked to come, we couldn't say no. She seemed so much better here and had a lot of what she called 'happy days'. But the last few weeks, she declined rapidly..." Her voice faltered. "She left something for you...if only I can find it. Could you wait a moment while I look?"

I nodded stupidly, my mind racing for something to say to this lovely young woman.

She handed me a smeared envelope with "Mr. P" printed in bold, childish letters. Inside was a drawing in bright crayon hues - a yellow beach, a blue sea and a brown bird. Underneath was carefully printed: A SANDPIPER TO BRING YOU JOY. Tears welled up in my eyes and a heart that had almost forgotten how to love opened wide. I took Wendy's mother in my arms. "I'm so sorry, I'm so sorry, I'm so sorry," I muttered over and over, and we wept together.

The precious little picture is framed now and hangs in my study. Six words - one for each year of her life - that speak to me of harmony, courage and undemanding love. A gift from a child with sea-blue eyes and hair the colour of sand, who taught me the gift of love.

By Mary Sherman Hilbert, published in the Reader's Digest in 1980.

Hilbert was not the one who had the encounter with the child; she was merely repeating a story she heard years earlier.

THE PASSENGER

The passengers on the bus watched sympathetically as the attractive young woman with the white cane made her way carefully up the steps. She paid the driver and, using her hands to feel the location of the seats, walked down the aisle and found the seat he'd told her was empty. Then she settled in, placed her briefcase on her lap and rested her cane against her leg.

It had been a year since Susan, 34, became blind. Due to a medical misdiagnosis, she had been rendered sightless, and she was suddenly thrown into a world of darkness, anger, frustration and self-pity. Once a normal woman, Susan now felt condemned by this terrible twist of fate to become a powerless, helpless burden on everyone around her. "How could this have happened to me?" she would plead, her heart knotted with anger. But no matter how much she cried or ranted or prayed, she knew the painful truth - her sight was never going to return. A cloud of depression hung over Susan's once optimistic spirit. Just getting through each day was an exercise in frustration and exhaustion. And all she had to cling to was her husband Mark.

Mark was an Air Force officer, and he loved Susan with all of his heart. When she first lost her sight, he watched her sink into despair and was determined to help his wife gain the strength and confidence she needed to become independent again. Mark's military background had trained him well to deal with sensitive situations, and yet he knew this was the most difficult battle he would ever face.

Finally, Susan felt ready to return to her job, but how would she get there? She used to take the bus, but was now too frightened to get around the city by herself. Mark volunteered to drive her to work each day, even though they worked at opposite ends of the city. At first, this comforted Susan and fulfilled Mark's need to protect his sightless wife, who was so insecure about performing the slightest task. Soon, however, Mark realised that this arrangement wasn't working - it was hectic, and costly. Susan is going to have to start taking the bus again, he admitted to himself. But just the thought of mentioning it to her made him cringe. She was still so fragile, so angry. How would she react?

Just as Mark predicted, Susan was horrified at the idea of taking the bus again. "I'm blind!" she responded bitterly. "How am I supposed to know where I'm going? I feel like you're abandoning me." Mark's heart broke to hear these words, but he knew what had to be done. He promised Susan that each morning and evening he would ride the bus with her, for as long as it took, until she got the hang of it. And that is exactly what happened.

For two solid weeks, Mark, military uniform and all, accompanied Susan to and from work each day. He taught her how to rely on her other senses, specifically her hearing, to determine where she was and how to adapt to her new environment. He helped her befriend the bus drivers who could watch out for her, and save her a seat. He made her laugh, even on those not-so-good days when she would trip exiting the bus, or drop her briefcase. Each morning, they made the journey together, and Mark would take a cab back to his office. Although this routine was even more costly and exhausting than the previous one, Mark knew it was only a matter of time before Susan would be able to ride the bus on her own. He believed in her, in the Susan he used to know before she'd lost her sight, who wasn't afraid of any challenge and who would never, ever quit.

Finally, Susan decided that she was ready to try the trip on her own. Monday morning arrived, and before she left, she threw her arms around Mark; her temporary bus riding companion, her husband and her best friend. Her eyes filled with tears of gratitude for his loyalty, his patience, his love. She said good-bye, and for the first time, they went their separate ways. Monday, Tuesday, Wednesday, Thursday ... Each day on her own went perfectly, and Susan had never felt better. She was doing it! She was going to work all by herself!

On Friday morning, Susan took the bus to work as usual. As she was paying for her fare to exit the bus, the driver said, "Boy, I sure envy you." Susan wasn't sure if the driver was speaking to her or not. After all, who on earth would ever envy a blind woman who had struggled just to find the courage to live for the past year? Curious, she asked the driver, "Why do you say that you envy me?"

The driver responded, "It must feel so good to be taken care of and protected like you are." Susan had no idea what the driver was talking about, and asked again, "What do you mean?"

The driver answered, "You know, every morning for the past week, a fine-looking gentleman in a military uniform has been standing across the corner watching you when you get off the bus. He makes sure you cross the street safely, and he watches you until you enter your office building. Then he blows you a kiss, gives you a little salute and walks away. You are one lucky lady!"

Tears of happiness poured down Susan's cheeks. For although she couldn't physically see him, she had always felt Mark's presence. She was blessed, so blessed, for he had given her a gift more powerful than sight, a gift she didn't need to see to believe - the gift of love that can bring light where there had been darkness.

Author Unknown

WHAT DOES LOVE MEAN?...
A CHILD'S DEFINITION

A group of teachers posed this question to a group of 4 to 8-year-olds: "What does love mean?" The answers they got were broader and deeper than anyone could have imagined. See what you think...

"When my grandmother got arthritis, she couldn't bend over and paint her toenails anymore. So my grandfather does it for her all the time, even when his hands got arthritis too. That's love." Rebecca - aged 8

"When someone loves you, the way they say your name is different. You know that your name is safe in their mouth." Billy - aged 4

"Love is when a girl puts on perfume and a boy puts on shaving cologne and they go out and smell each other." Karl - aged 5

"Love is when you go out to eat and give somebody most of your French fries without making them give you any of theirs." Chrissy - aged 6

"Love is what makes you smile when you're tired." Terri - aged 4

"Love is when my mommy makes coffee for my daddy and she takes a sip before giving it to him, to make sure the taste is OK." Danny - aged 7

"Love is when you kiss all the time. Then when you get tired of kissing, you still want to be together and you talk more. My Mommy and Daddy are like that. They look gross when they kiss!" Emily - aged 8

"Love is what's in the room with you at Christmas if you stop opening presents and listen." Bobby - aged 7 (Wow!)

"If you want to learn to love better, you should start with a friend who you hate." Nikka - aged 6

"There are two kinds of love. Our love and God's love. But God makes both kinds of them." Jenny - aged 8

"Love is when you tell a guy you like his shirt, then he wears it every day." Noelle - aged 7

"Love is like a little old woman and a little old man who are still friends even after they know each other so well." Tommy - aged 6

"During my piano recital, I was on a stage and I was scared. I looked at all the people watching me and saw my daddy waving and smiling. He was the only one doing that. I wasn't scared anymore." Cindy - aged 8

"My mommy loves me more than anybody. You don't see anyone else kissing me to sleep at night." Clare - aged 6

"Love is when Mommy gives Daddy the best piece of chicken." Elaine - aged 5

"Love is when Mommy sees Daddy smelly and sweaty and still says he is handsomer than Robert Redford." Chris - age 7

"Love is when your puppy licks your face even after you left him alone all day." Mary Ann - aged 4

"I know my older sister loves me because she gives me all her old clothes and has to go out and buy new ones." Lauren - aged 4

"When you love somebody, your eyelashes go up and down and little stars come out of you." Karen - aged 7

"Love is when Mommy sees Daddy on the toilet and she doesn't think it's gross." Mark - aged 6

"You really shouldn't say 'I love you' unless you mean it. But if you mean it, you should say it a lot. People forget." Jessica - aged 8

■ ■ ■

THE CONTEST

A famous author and lecturer once talked about a contest he was asked to judge.

The purpose of the contest was to find the most caring child. The winner was a four-year old child whose next-door neighbour was an elderly gentleman who had recently lost his wife.

Upon seeing the man cry, the little boy went into the old gentleman's yard, climbed onto his lap and just sat there. When his Mother asked him what he had said to the neighbour, the little boy said:

"Nothing, I just helped him cry."

By Leo Buscaglia, motivational speaker

HOW TO DANCE IN THE RAIN

It was 8:30 on a very busy morning at the hospital, when an elderly gentleman in his eighties arrived to have stitches removed from his thumb. He said he was in a hurry as he had an appointment at 9:00 am.

I took his vital signs and had him take a seat, knowing it would be more than an hour before someone would be able to see him. I saw him looking at his watch and decided, since I was not busy with another patient, that I would evaluate his wound. On exam, it was well healed, so I talked

197

to one of the doctors, and got the necessary supplies to remove his sutures and redress his wound.

While taking care of his wound, I asked him if he had another doctor's appointment this morning, as he was in such a hurry. The gentleman told me no, that he needed to go to the nursing home to eat breakfast with his wife. I inquired about her health.

He told me that she had been there for a while and that she was a victim of Alzheimer's disease. As we talked, I asked if she would be upset if he was a bit late.

He replied that she no longer knew who he was, that she had not recognised him in five years. I was surprised, and asked him, "And you still go every morning, even though she doesn't know who you are?"

He smiled as he patted my hand and said, "She doesn't know me, but I still know who she is."

I had to hold back tears as he left. I had goose bumps on my arm, and thought, 'that's the kind of love I want in my life.'

True love is neither physical, nor romantic. True love is an acceptance of all that is, has been, will be and will not be.

The happiest people don't necessarily have the best of everything; they just make the best of everything they have.

Author Unknown

CHAPTER SIXTEEN :
MAKING ASSUMPTIONS

THE PILOT

Tom was told that a certain plane would be waiting for him at noon at the airport.

Arriving at the spot, he saw a plane warming up just outside the hanger.

He greeted the pilot, jumped in, and without asking anything, he said, "Let's go." The pilot took off.

When in the air, Tom said to the pilot, "Fly low over the mountain so I can take pictures of the hill."

The pilot replied, "Why?"

Tom answered, "Because I'm the photographer for BBC news. I want to take some close-up shots."

The pilot was silent for a moment. Then he stammered, "So you're not my flying instructor?"

Author Unknown

THE COOKIE THIEF

A woman was waiting at an airport one night
   With several long hours before her flight,
She hunted for a book in the airport shop,
Bought a bag of cookies and found a place to drop.

She was engrossed in her book but happened to see
That the man beside her, as bold as could be,
Grabbed a cookie or two from the bag between
Which she tried to ignore to avoid a scene.

She munched cookies and watched the clock
As the gutsy cookie thief diminished her stock.
She was getting more irritated as the minutes ticked by
Thinking "If I wasn't so nice I'd blacken his eye!"

With each cookie she took, he took one too
When only one was left, she wondered what he'd do.
With a smile on his face and a nervous laugh
He took the last cookie and broke it in half.

He offered her half as he ate the other,
She snatched it from him and thought
"Oh Brother, this guy has some nerve and he's also
Rude, why he didn't even show any gratitude!"

She had never known when she had been so galled
And sighed with relief when her flight was called.
She gathered her belongings and headed to the gate
Refusing to look back at the thieving ingrate.

She boarded the plane and sank in her seat
And sought her book which was almost complete.

As she reached in her bag she gasped with surprise
There was her bag of cookies in front of her eyes!

"If mine are here" she moaned with despair
"Then the others were his and he tried to share!"
Too late to apologise she realised with grief
That she was the rude one, the ingrate, the thief.

By Valerie Cox

* * *

THE JOB INTERVIEW

Back when the telegraph was the fastest method of long-distance communication, a young man applied for a job as a Morse code operator. Answering an ad in the newspaper, he went to the office address that was listed. When he arrived, he entered a large, busy office filled with noise and clatter, including the sound of the telegraph in the background. A sign on the receptionist's counter instructed job applicants to fill out a form and wait until they were summoned to enter the inner office.

The young man filled out his form and sat down with the seven other applicants in the waiting area. After a few minutes, the young man stood up, crossed the room to the door of the inner office, and walked right in. Naturally the other applicants perked up, wondering what was going on. They muttered among themselves that they hadn't heard any summons yet.

They assumed that the young man who went into the office made a mistake and would be disqualified. Within a few minutes, however, the employer escorted the young man out of the office and said to the other applicants, "Ladies and Gentlemen, thank you very much for coming, but the job has just been filled." The other applicants began grumbling to each other, and one spoke up saying, "Wait a minute, I don't understand. He was the last to come in, and we never even got a chance to be interviewed. Yet he got the job. That's not fair!"

The employer said, "I'm sorry, but the last several minutes while you've been sitting here, the telegraph has been ticking out the following message in Morse code: 'If you understand this message, then come right in. The job is yours.' None of you heard it or understood it. This young man did. Therefore, the job is his."

Adapted from various versions on the internet

A FLIGHT TO CATCH

A man and his wife had been arguing all night, and as bedtime approached neither was speaking to the other. It was not unusual for the pair to continue this war of silence for two or three days but on this occasion, the man was concerned because he needed to be awake at 4.30am the next morning to catch an important flight. Being a very heavy sleeper, he usually relied on his wife to wake him.

While his wife was in the bathroom, he wrote on a post-it note: "Please wake me at 4.30am - I have an important flight to catch". He put the post-it note on his wife's pillow, then turned over and went to sleep.

The man awoke the next morning and looked at the clock. It was 8.00am. Furious that he had missed his flight, he was about to go in search of his errant wife to give her a piece of his mind, when he spotted a hand-written post-it note on his bedside cabinet.

The note said: "It's 4.30 - get up."

Author Unknown

THE HANDWRITING ON THE WALL

A weary mother returned from the store,
    Lugging groceries through the kitchen door.
Awaiting her arrival was her eight-year-old son,
Anxious to relate what his younger brother had done.

203

"While I was out playing and Dad was on a call,
T.J. took his crayons and wrote on the wall!
It's on the new paper you just hung in the den.
I told him you'd be mad at having to do it again."

She let out a moan and furrowed her brow,
"Where is your little brother right now?"
She emptied her arms and with a purposeful stride,
She marched to his closet where he had gone to hide.

She called his full name as she entered his room.
He trembled with fear--he knew that meant doom!
For the next ten minutes, she ranted and raved
About the expensive wallpaper and how she had saved.

Lamenting all the work it would take to repair,
She condemned his actions and total lack of care.
The more she scolded, the madder she got,
Then stomped from his room, totally distraught!

She headed for the den to confirm her fears.
When she saw the wall, her eyes flooded with tears.
The message she read pierced her soul with a dart.
It said, "I love Mommy," surrounded by a heart.

Well, the wallpaper remained, just as she found it,
With an empty picture frame hung to surround it.
A reminder to her, and indeed to all,
Take time to read the handwriting on the wall.

Author Unknown

THE TRAMP

It's November, around 6.00pm, and there's a tramp sitting near Victoria Station in London. It's getting dark, starting to rain, and it's pretty cold. It's busy with commuters rushing to go home, all in their suits with briefcases, walking quickly.

The tramp is sitting there with his dog, and looks up to see a business man walk out of the pizza restaurant opposite, and cross the busy road carrying a pizza box. He comes up to the tramp, smiles, and holds out the pizza box. "Hey, I got this for you."

The tramp looks up, smiles, and says "Thanks, but no thanks".

The man looks at the tramp, a bit confused, "No, you don't understand, it's not the remains of my pizza. I was sitting in the window there eating when I saw you, and I thought it's going to be a long cold night, so I asked them to make this pizza for you to take away - it's a Margarita."

The tramp shakes his head, "It's really kind of you, and I'm sure one of the other guys would love it, but I don't eat pizza".

The man is a bit confused now, and actually quite annoyed. "What do you mean you don't eat pizza?" He sees the tramp living on the street with nothing and it doesn't make sense. "What do you eat?" he asks.

The tramp looks up. "There's a door down that street that's at the back of a supermarket; every evening at around

10.00pm they bring out all the fruit and veg that can't be sold and they are happy for me to have as much as I like."

Now the man is very confused. "So you won't eat this freshly made hot pizza, but you will eat the old fruit and veg? Why would you want to do that?"

The tramp explains, "Well, if I don't look after my body, I'll have nowhere to live!"

We all have a home, some more than one, but we only have one body - and if we don't look after it, we'll have nowhere to live.

A motivational story by Fran Wallis told at a Yoga Retreat in Turkey

---

NEVER PREJUDGE

A lady in a faded gingham dress and her husband, dressed in a homespun threadbare suit, stepped off the train in Boston and walked timidly, without an appointment, into the Harvard president's outer office. The secretary could tell in a moment that such backwoods, country hicks had no business at Harvard and probably didn't even deserve to be in Cambridge. She frowned.

"We want to see the president," the man said softly.

"He'll be busy all day," the secretary snapped. "We'll wait," the lady replied.

For hours, the secretary ignored them, hoping that the couple would finally become discouraged and go away. They didn't. And the secretary grew frustrated and finally decided to disturb the president, even though it was a chore she was always reluctant to do. "Maybe if they just see you for a few minutes, they'll leave," she told him. The president sighed in exasperation and nodded. Someone of his importance obviously didn't have the time to spend with them, but he detested gingham dresses and homespun suits cluttering up his outer office. The president, stern-faced with dignity, strutted toward the couple.

The lady told him, "We had a son that attended Harvard for one year. He loved Harvard. He was happy here. But about a year ago, he was accidentally killed. And my husband and I would like to erect a memorial to him, somewhere on campus." The president was astonished.

"Madam," he said gruffly, "we can't put up a statue for every person who attended Harvard and died. If we did, this place would look like a cemetery."

"Oh, no," the lady explained quickly, "we don't want to erect a statue. We thought we would like to give a building to Harvard."

The president rolled his eyes. He glanced at the gingham dress and homespun suit, then exclaimed, "A building! Do you have any earthly idea how much a building costs? We have over seven and a half million dollars in property at Harvard." For a moment the lady was silent. The president was pleased. He could get rid of them now.

The lady turned to her husband and said quietly, "Is that all it costs to start a University? Why don't we just start our own?" Her husband nodded. The president's face wilted in confusion and bewilderment.

Mr. and Mrs. Leland Stanford walked away, travelling on to Palo Alto, California, where they established the University that bears their name, and stands as a memorial to a son that Harvard no longer cared about!

Adapted from various versions on the internet

CHAPTER SEVENTEEN : PARENTING

A LIFE LESSON FROM A BABY GIRAFFE

Baby giraffes never go to school. But they learn a very important lesson rather early in life, a lesson that we all can learn from.

The birth of a baby giraffe is quite an earth-shaking event. The baby falls from its mother's womb, some eight feet above the ground. It shrivels up and lies still, too weak to move.

The mother giraffe lovingly lowers her neck to smooch the baby giraffe. And then something incredible happens. She lifts one of her long legs and kicks the baby giraffe, sending it flying up in the air and tumbling back down to the ground. As the baby lies curled up, the mother kicks the baby again. And again, until the baby giraffe, still trembling and tired, pushes its limbs and for the first time, learns to stand on its feet.

Happy to see the baby standing on its own feet, the mother giraffe comes over and gives it yet another kick. The baby giraffe falls one more time, but now quickly recovers and stands up. Mother Giraffe is delighted.

She knows that her baby has learnt an important lesson; she wants it to remember how it got up.

Why does the mother giraffe do this?

She knows that in the wild, baby giraffes must be able to get up as quickly as possible to stay with the herd, where there is safety. Lions, hyenas, leopards and wild hunting dogs all enjoy eating young giraffes. So unless the baby giraffe quickly learns to stand and run with the pack – it will have no chance of survival.

Adapted from various versions on the internet.

A FATHER'S HEARTFELT WORDS

My twenty-three-year-old son Dan stood in the doorway, ready to say goodbye to his home. His rucksack was packed and ready for the journey. In a couple of hours, he was going to fly out to France. He was going to be away for at least a year to learn a new language and experience life in a foreign country.

It was a milestone in Dan's life, a transition from school days to adulthood. When we were ready to say goodbye, I looked closely at his face. I wanted like to provide him with some good advice that would last longer than just here and now.

But not a sound came from my lips. There was nothing that broke the silence in our house by the sea. I could hear the sharp cry of the seagulls outside, while they circled over the ever-changing and roaring surf. Inside, I stood motionless and silent, looking into my son's green eyes with a penetrating look.

I knew that this wasn't the first time I let such an opportunity pass me by, and that made everything even more difficult. When Daniel was a little boy, I followed him to the bus on his first day in preschool. I felt the excitement in the hand that held mine when the bus came around the corner. I saw the colour spread in his cheeks when the bus stopped. He looked at me - just like he did now.

"What's it like, Dad? Can I do it? Will I do all right?" And then he boarded the bus and disappeared. The bus drove away. And I hadn't said a word.

Some ten years later, a similar episode took place. His mother and I drove him to the university where he was going to study. On the first night he went out with his new friends and when we met the next morning, he threw up. He was sick with glandular fever, but we thought he had a hangover.

Dan was ill in bed in his room when I wanted to say goodbye. I tried to come up with something to say, something that could inspire courage and self-confidence in him in this new era of his life.

Again, the words let me down. I mumbled something like "I hope you're better, Dan." Then I turned around and left.

Now I stood in front him and recalled all the times when I hadn't made use of those opportunities. How often has that not happened to all of us? A son graduates or a daughter is married. We do what has to be done at those kinds of ceremonies, but we don't pull our children aside to tell them what they have meant to us. Or what they might expect of the future.

There was one chance I didn't miss, however. One day I told Dan that the biggest mistake in my life was that I had not taken a year's sabbatical after I graduated from university. I could have travelled around the world, but I married, began working and the dream about living in another culture soon had to be shelved.

Dan thought about what I had said. His friends told him he was crazy to put off his career. But he quickly realised that it probably wasn't a bad idea. And after he graduated from university, he worked as a waiter, a messenger and an assistant in a bookstore, so he could make enough money to go to Paris.

The night before his departure, I lay twisting and turning in bed, puzzling about what to tell him. I couldn't think of anything. Maybe, I thought, it wasn't really necessary after all. Seen in the perspective of an entire life, how important is it that a father tells his son what he thinks of him, deep inside?

But when I stood in front of Dan, I knew that it really did mean something. My father and I were fond of each other, and yet I have always felt sorry that he never expressed his feelings for me in words, that I didn't have a memory of such a moment. Now I felt my palms becoming moist, and my throat draw together. Why does it have to be so difficult to tell your son what you feel? My mouth was dry, and I knew that I could only say a few words.

"Dan," I finally stammered out, "if I had the choice myself, I would have chosen you."

That was all I could say. I was not sure he understood what I meant. But then he stepped towards me and put his arms around me. For a short while the world and everything in it disappeared; there was only Dan and me in our home by the sea.

He was about to say something, but my eyes welled up and I didn't catch what he said. I only noticed his stubble pressing against my face. Then the moment was over. I went to work and a couple of hours later, Dan took off with his girlfriend.

It all happened a while ago. I think about him when I walk along the beach. Many miles away he may be hurrying across Boulevard Saint-Germain, strolling through the halls of the Louvre or having a drink at a café on the Left Bank of the Seine.

What I told Dan was clumsy and commonplace. It was nothing. And yet, it was everything.

By David Zinman

■ ■ ■

LEARNING TO LISTEN

We all know what it's like to get that phone call in the middle of the night. This night's call was no different.

Jerking up to the ringing summons, I focused on the red illuminated numbers of my clock. Midnight. Panicky thoughts filled my sleep-dazed mind as I grabbed the receiver.

"Hello?"

My heart pounded; I gripped the phone tighter and eyed my husband, who was now turning to face my side of the bed.

"Mama?"

I could hardly hear the whisper over the static. But my thoughts immediately went to my daughter. When the desperate sound of a young, crying voice became clearer on the line, I grabbed for my husband and squeezed his wrist.

"Mama, I know it's late, but don't...don't say anything, until I finish. And before you ask, yes, I've been drinking. I nearly ran off the road a few miles back and..."

I drew in a sharp, shallow breath, released my husband's wrist and pressed my hand against my forehead. Sleep still fogged my mind, and I attempted to fight back the panic.

Something wasn't right.

"And I got so scared. All I could think about was how it would hurt you if a policeman came to your door and said I'd been killed. I want...to come home. I know running away was wrong. I know you've been worried sick. I should have called you days ago, but I was afraid...afraid..."

Sobs of deep-felt emotion flowed from the receiver and poured into my heart. Immediately, I pictured my daughter's face in my mind and my fogged senses seemed to clear. "I think..."

"No! Please let me finish! Please!" She pleaded, not so much in anger but in desperation.

I paused and tried to think of what to say. Before I could go on, she continued, "I'm pregnant, Mama. I know I shouldn't be drinking now... especially now, but I'm scared, Mama, so scared!"

The voice broke again and I bit my lip feeling my own eyes fill with moisture. I looked at my husband who sat silently mouthing, "Who is it?"

I shook my head and when I didn't answer, he jumped up and left the room, returning seconds later with the portable phone held to his ear. She must have heard the click in the line because she continued, "Are you still there? Please don't hang up on me! I need you. I feel so alone."

I clutched the phone and stared at my husband, seeking guidance. "I'm here, I wouldn't hang up," I said.

"I know I should have told you, Mama. But when we talk, you just keep telling me what I should do. You read all those pamphlets on how to talk about sex and all, but all you do is talk. You don't listen to me. You never let me tell you how I feel. It's as if my feelings aren't important. Because you're my mother, you think you have all the answers. But sometimes I don't need answers. I just want someone to listen."

I swallowed the lump in my throat and stared at the 'how-to-talk-to-your-kids' pamphlets scattered on my nightstand. "I'm listening," I whispered.

"You know, back there on the road, after I got the car under control, I started thinking about the baby and taking care of it. Then I saw this phone booth and it was as if I could hear you preaching about how people shouldn't drink and drive. So I called a taxi. I want to come home."

"That's good, Honey," I said, as relief filled my chest. My husband came closer, sat down beside me and laced his fingers through mine. I knew from his touch that he thought I was doing and saying the right thing.

"But you know, I think I can drive now."

"No!" I snapped. My muscles stiffened, and I tightened the clasp on my husband's hand. "Please, wait for the taxi. Don't hang up on me until the taxi gets there."

"I just want to come home, Mama."

"I know. But do this for your mama. Wait for the taxi, please." I listened to the silence in fear. When I didn't hear her answer, I bit my lip and closed my eyes. Somehow I had to stop her from driving.

"There's the taxi, now."

Only when I heard someone in the background asking about a Yellow Cab did I feel my tension easing.

"I'm coming home, Mama."

There was a click and the phone went silent. Moving from the bed with tears forming in my eyes, I walked out into the hall and went to stand in my sixteen-year-old daughter's room. The dark silence hung thick. My husband came from behind, wrapped his arms around me and rested his chin on the top of my head. I wiped the tears from my cheeks.

"We have to learn to listen," I said.

He pulled me around to face him. "We'll learn. You'll see."

Then he took me into his arms and I buried my head in his shoulder. I let him hold me for several moments, and then I pulled back and stared back at the bed. He studied me for a second, and asked, "Do you think she'll ever know she dialled the wrong number?"

I looked at our sleeping daughter, then back at him. "Maybe it wasn't such a wrong number."

"Mom, Dad, what are you doing?" The muffled young voice came from under the covers.

I walked over to my daughter, who now sat up staring into the darkness.

"We're practicing," I answered.

"Practicing what?" she mumbled and laid back on the mattress, her eyes already closed in slumber.

"Listening," I whispered, and brushed a hand over her cheek.

By Johnny Silvas

DAD

"I didn't take your cigarettes!" I half yelled, rudely.

"OK, whatever...," said the deep, grouchy voice I knew too well.

"OK, well I'm going," I said dryly.

"Aaa-lright."

And with the click of the telephone I turned away and headed off to be with some friends.

Moments before I had learned that my mother, sister, brother and step-father were leaving to go on vacation without me. In a terrible fit of jealousy, I let my displeasure be known. I went on and on about how messed up it was that I was not invited and how my family did not love me. Just on and on. This rode well into the next day.

July 16,1999 is my step-father's 50th birthday. It was going to be his first birthday party ever. My mother had told me two or three times, so I was well aware. I had planned to be there at my dad's first birthday party (even though ever since I had hit adolescence, we had never seen eye to eye and fought constantly), but in the 'situation' I thought he had put me in, and in my moment of pure selfishness and resentfulness, I decided to say I'd show and just not go.

All the better, my friend Kelly called and asked me to go with her to her family reunion... a perfect excuse! So at about ten that night I called home. It was busy so I left a voicemail message: "Mom I left your shorts at Aunt Sheila's. If you want them before you leave on vacation tomorrow, you'd better go get them."

No 'I love you'.

No 'be careful'.

No 'tell dad happy birthday'.

All the way to Ohio with Kelly, I bad-mouthed him and my mom for marrying him. I felt so angry and left out. I blamed it all on him. It was always Denny's fault. I just knew he had been the one to suggest not taking me. We never got along, it seemed.

Eventually, we arrived at our destination and tucked in for the night. I never thought twice about my family. Never once thought of all the fun they were probably having at Denny's birthday party. Not once about the excitement they all had for leaving on vacation tomorrow. I only thought of myself.

The next morning, after I had got ready, we hit the road to meet the rest of Kelly's family at an all-day reunion. We stopped at K-mart. One of Kelly's relatives pulled up to the car.

"Jara, you need to call home - something bad happened," she said.

"What?" I asked. "Who?"

"Your step-dad had a heart attack or something," she replied.

"Is he OK?" I said quietly, as I began to shake.

"I don't know, you'll have to call," and she drove away.

I got out of the car, headed towards a nearby telephone booth. I called. My mom's voice came over the line.

"Jara...," mom said, meekly.

"Mom, what happened, are you OK?" I asked.

"Denny's dead ... come home, please Jara, come home."

"OK mom, I'll be there," I said quietly. "I love you."

My legs were rubber, I couldn't talk, and tears were flooding my eyes and running down my face.

That night at his birthday party, after the guests had left, Denny had suffered a massive heart attack. It was caused from emphysema and heart disease that he never even knew about. He died in my mother's arms.

You see, I never made peace with Denny. I never took the time to show how really important to me he was. I never took the time to tell him he was my Daddy.

He had been there when my biological dad hadn't. He was the one who clothed, fed and sheltered me as long as I can remember. He was the one that rubbed my belly for hours when I was home sick from school. He was the one who helped me move into my first apartment. He was the one that tried, till his deathbed, to give me values and responsibility. He was the one man I knew in my life who would love me unconditionally. I never told him how much all that meant to me. I never told him that he was my Daddy.

After all this, I've learned it so important not to let things go unsaid, no matter how minor or major. Even though I know Denny knew I loved him, I would feel so much better knowing he knew for sure, because I hurt him in so many ways. And you see, despite all that, he never once complained.

By Jara Crawford

DON'T HOPE...DECIDE!

While waiting to pick up a friend at the airport in Portland, Oregon, I had one of those life-changing experiences that you hear other people talk about - the kind that sneaks up on you unexpectedly. This one occurred a mere two feet away from me.

Straining to locate my friend among the passengers disembarking through the jet way, I noticed a man coming toward me carrying two light bags. He stopped right next to me to greet his family.

First, he motioned to his youngest son (maybe six years old) as he laid down his bags. They gave each other a long, loving hug. As they separated enough to look in each other's face, I heard the father say, "It's so good to see you, son. I missed you so much!" His son smiled somewhat shyly, averted his eyes and replied softly, "Me too, Dad!"

Then the man stood up, gazed in the eyes of his oldest son (maybe nine or ten), and while cupping his son's face in his hands said, "You're already quite the young man. I love you very much, Zach!" They too hugged, a most loving, tender hug.

While this was happening, a baby girl (perhaps one or one-and-a-half) was squirming excitedly in her mother's arms, never once taking her little eyes off the wonderful sight of her returning father. The man said, "Hi, baby girl!" as he gently took the child from her mother. He quickly kissed her face all over and then held her close to his chest while rocking her from side to side. The little girl instantly relaxed and simply laid her head on his shoulder, motionless in pure contentment.

After several moments, he handed his daughter to his oldest son and declared, "I've saved the best for last!" He proceeded to give his wife the longest, most passionate kiss I ever remember seeing. He gazed into her eyes for several seconds and then silently mouthed, "I love you so much!" They stared into each other's eyes, beaming big smiles at one another, while holding both hands.

For an instant they reminded me of newlyweds, but I knew by the age of their kids that they couldn't possibly be. I puzzled about it for a moment then realised how totally engrossed I was in this wonderful display of unconditional love not more than an arm's length away from me. I suddenly felt uncomfortable, as if I was invading something sacred, but was amazed to hear my own voice nervously ask, "Wow! How long have you two been married?"

"Been together fourteen years total, married twelve of those," he replied, without breaking his gaze from his lovely wife's face.

"Well then, how long have you been away?" I asked.

The man finally turned and looked at me, still beaming his joyous smile. "Two whole days!"

Two days?! I was stunned. By the intensity of the greeting, I had assumed he'd been gone for at least several weeks - if not months! I know my expression betrayed me. Almost offhandedly, hoping to end my intrusion with some semblance of grace (and to get back to searching for my friend), I said, "I hope my marriage is still that passionate after twelve years!"

The man suddenly stopped smiling.

He looked me straight in the eye, and with a forcefulness that burned right into my soul, he told me something that left me a different person. He told me, "Don't hope, friend... decide!" Then he flashed me his wonderful smile again, shook my hand and said, "God bless!"

By Michael D. Hargrove

LITTLE EYES UPON YOU

There are little eyes upon you
That watch you day and night.
There are little ears that quickly take in every word that you say.

There are little hands all eager to do anything you do
And a little child who is dreaming of the day they will be like you

You are the little one's idol
The wisest of the wise.
In their little minds no suspicions ever rise about you
They believe in you devoutly
And hold all you say and do
So that they may do the same when they are grown up just like you.

There is a wide eyed little one
Who believes you are always right

And their eyes are always open, watching you day and night.
You are setting an example every day in all you do
For the little one who is waiting to grow up to be just like you.

Based on a poem by Avleek Dhiman

CHAPTER EIGHTEEN : PERSISTENCE

THE CHINESE BAMBOO TREE

There is a Chinese bamboo tree that thrives in Indonesia. Planting, watering and fertilising the seed for five years yields no visual results, but shortly after that the tree sprouts and grows to over ninety feet in around five weeks!

Now the question is, does it grow 90 feet tall in five weeks, or five years? The answer is obvious. It grows 90 feet tall in five years. Because at any time, had that person stopped watering and nurturing and fertilizing that seed, that bamboo tree would've died in the ground.

■ ■ ■

THE JUDO CHAMPION

There was a ten-year-old boy who tragically lost his left arm in a car accident. The boy's father wanted him to regain confidence in himself so he encouraged him to begin taking judo lessons. His Sensei was a Japanese Judo Master. The master trained the boy every day for weeks. Each day, they would go through the same training routine and the Sensei trained the boy on the same throw. Over and over, they practiced the same move.

One day the boy asked, "Master, shouldn't I be learning more moves?"

The Sensei responded, "This is the only move you will ever need to know."

Several months later, the master entered the boy in his first Judo tournament. The boy was nervous but eager to test his skills. To his surprise, he easily won his first match. The second opponent was more difficult but still rather easy for the one-armed boy. After winning the first two matches, he qualified for the semi-finals. His opponent was the toughest yet. The boy still won. Finally, he entered the last match. At the start he could tell his opponent was much more experienced. It was one sided for most of the match. The boy's father was watching from the stands and he was growing more and more concerned. The dad told the Sensei, "He's not ready for this; this is too hard." The Sensei stayed silent and watched. He was confident the boy would be victorious, and if he lost he could accept that too. After a hard-fought battle, the boy won and his hand was raised. He bowed to his opponent and walked off the mat.

On the ride home, the boy asked, "Sensei, how did I win my first Judo tournament with only one move?"

The master looked at him and said: "You won for two reasons. First, you've mastered the most difficult throw in Judo. And second, the only known defence for the move is for the opponent to grab your left arm..."

And so, the boy's biggest weakness had become his biggest strength.

Adapted from various versions on the internet

ADRIFT

In 1982, Steven Callahan was crossing the Atlantic alone in his sailboat, when it struck something and sank. He was out of the shipping lanes and floating in a life- raft, alone. His supplies were few. His chances were small. Yet when three fishermen found him seventy-six days later (the longest anyone has survived a shipwreck on a life-raft alone), he was alive; much skinnier than he was when he started, but alive.

His account of how he survived is fascinating. His ingenuity - how he managed to catch fish, how he fixed his solar still (which distils salt sea water to make fresh) - is very interesting.

But the thing that caught my eye was how he managed to keep himself going when all hope seemed lost. There seemed no point in continuing the struggle when his suffering was so great; his life-raft was punctured and after more than a week struggling with his weak body to fix it, it was still leaking air - and wearing him out to keep pumping it up. He was starved. He was desperately dehydrated. He was thoroughly exhausted. Giving up would have seemed the only sane option.

When people survive these kinds of circumstances, they do something with their minds that gives them the courage to keep going. Many people in similarly desperate situations give in or go mad. Yet something the survivors do with their thoughts helps them find the guts to carry on, in spite of overwhelming odds.

"I tell myself I can handle it," wrote Callahan in his narrative. "Compared to what others have been through,

I'm fortunate. I tell myself these things over and over, building up fortitude..."

I wrote that down after I read it. It struck me as something important. And I've told myself the same thing when my own goals seemed far off or when my problems seemed too overwhelming. And every time I've said it, I have always come back to my senses.

The truth is, our circumstances are only bad compared to something better. But others have been through much worse. I've read enough history to know that you and I are lucky to be where we are, when we are - no matter how bad things seem to us compared to our fantasies. It's a sane thought, and worth thinking.

So here, coming to us from the extreme edge of survival, are words that can give us strength: "Whatever you're going through, tell yourself you can handle it. Compared to what others have been through, you're fortunate. Tell this to yourself over and over, and it will help you get through the rough spots with a little more fortitude nonetheless!"

By Adam Khan

THE RACE

Whenever I start to hang my head in front of failure's face,
my downward fall is broken by the memory of a race.

A children's race, young boys, young men;
how I remember well,
  excitement sure, but also fear, it wasn't hard to tell.
They all lined up so full of hope, each thought to win that race
  or tie for first, or if not that, at least take second place.
Their parents watched from off the side,
  each cheering for their son,
  and each boy hoped to show his folks
that he would be the one.

The whistle blew and off they flew, like chariots of fire,
  to win, to be the hero there, was each young boy's desire.
One boy in particular, whose dad was in the crowd, was
  running in the lead and thought, "My dad will be so proud."
But as he speeded down the field and crossed a shallow dip,
  the little boy who thought he'd win, lost his step and slipped.
Trying hard to catch himself, his arms flew everyplace,
  and midst the laughter of the crowd he fell flat on his face.
As he fell, his hope fell too; he couldn't win it now.
  Humiliated, he just wished to disappear somehow.

But as he fell his dad stood up and showed his anxious face,
  which to the boy so clearly said, "Get up and win that race!"
He quickly rose, no damage done, behind a bit, that's all,
  and ran with all his mind and might to make up for his fall.
So anxious to restore himself, to catch up and to win, his
  mind went faster than his legs. He slipped and fell again.
He wished that he had quit before with only one disgrace.
  "I'm hopeless as a runner now, I shouldn't try to race."

229

But through the laughing crowd he searched and found his
father's face
    with a steady look that said again, "Get up and win that race!"
    So, he jumped up to try again, ten yards behind the last.
    "If I'm to gain those yards," he thought,
    "I've got to run real fast!"
Exceeding everything he had, he regained eight, then ten...
    but trying hard to catch the lead, he slipped and fell again.
Defeat! He lay there silently. A tear dropped from his eye.
    "There's no sense running anymore!
    Three strikes I'm out! Why try?
I've lost, so what's the use?" he thought.
"I'll live with my disgrace."
    But then he thought about his dad,
    who soon he'd have to face.

"Get up," an echo sounded low, "you haven't lost at all,
    for all you have to do to win is rise each time you fall.
Get up!" the echo urged him on, "Get up and take your place!
    You were not meant for failure here!
    Get up and win that race!"
So, up he rose to run once more, refusing to forfeit,
    and he resolved that win or lose, at least he wouldn't quit.
So far behind the others now, the most he'd ever been,
    still he gave it all he had and ran like he could win.
Three times he'd fallen stumbling, three times he rose again.
    Too far behind to hope to win, he still ran to the end.

They cheered another boy who crossed
the line and won first place,
    head high and proud and happy - no falling, no disgrace.
But, when the fallen youngster crossed the line, in last place,
    the crowd gave him a greater cheer for finishing the race.
And even though he came in last with

head bowed low, unproud,
 you would have thought he'd won the race,
 to listen to the crowd.
And to his dad he sadly said, "I didn't do so well."
 "To me, you won," his father said.
 "You rose each time you fell."

And now when things seem dark and
bleak and difficult to face,
 the memory of that little boy helps me in my own race.
For all of life is like that race, with ups and downs and all.
 And all you have to do to win is rise each time you fall.
And when depression and despair shout loudly in my face,
 another voice within me says, "Get up and win that race!"

Attributed to Dr. D.H. "Dee" Groberg

THE LOSER WHO NEVER GAVE UP

When he was a little boy his uncle called him "Sparky", after a comic-strip horse named Spark Plug. School was all but impossible for Sparky.

He failed every subject in the eighth grade. He flunked physics in high school, getting a grade of zero. He also flunked Latin, Algebra and English. And his record in sports wasn't any better. Though he did manage to make the school's golf team, he promptly lost the only important match of the season. Oh, there was a consolation match; he lost that too.

Throughout his youth, Sparky was awkward socially. It wasn't that the other students disliked him; it's just that no one really cared all that much. In fact, Sparky was astonished if a classmate ever said hello to him outside of school hours. There's no way to tell how he might have done at dating. He never once asked a girl out in high school. He was too afraid of being turned down... or perhaps laughed at. Sparky was a loser. He, his classmates... everyone knew it. So he learned to live with it. He made up his mind early that if things were meant to work out, they would. Otherwise he would content himself with what appeared to be his inevitable mediocrity.

One thing WAS important to Sparky, however, and that was drawing. He was proud of his artwork. No one else appreciated it. But that didn't seem to matter to him. In his senior year of high school, he submitted some cartoons to the yearbook. The editors rejected the concept. Despite this brush-off, Sparky was convinced of his ability. He even decided to become an artist.

So, after completing high school, Sparky wrote Walt Disney Studios. They asked for samples of his artwork. Despite careful preparation, this too was rejected. It was just one more confirmation that he was a loser.

But Sparky still didn't give up. Instead, he decided to tell his own life's story in cartoons. The main character would be a little boy who symbolised the perpetual loser and chronic underachiever. You know him well. Because Sparky's cartoon character went on to become a cultural phenomenon of sorts. People readily identified with this "lovable loser." He reminded people of the painful and embarrassing moments from their own past, of their pain and their shared humanity.

The character soon became famous worldwide: 'Charlie Brown.' And Sparky, the boy whose many failures never kept him from trying, whose work was rejected again and again, is the highly successful cartoonist, Charles Schultz. His cartoon strip, 'Peanuts,' continues to inspire children and adults with books, T-shirts and TV programmes, reminding us, as someone once commented, that life somehow finds a way for all of us - even the losers.

Sparky's story reminds us of a very important principle in life. We all face difficulty and discouragement from time to time. We also have a choice in how we handle it. If we're persistent, if we hold fast to our faith, if we continue to develop our unique talents, who knows what can happen? We may end up with an insight and an ability to inspire, one that only comes only through hardship.

Adapted from various versions on the internet

DREAMS OF GOLD

The Mel Fisher Story

Mel Fisher was born in Hobart, Indiana in 1922. After serving in World War II he moved to California and bought a chicken farm. It was there that Mel found the two loves of his life: his wife Dolores, whom he called Deo, and diving. In 1953 Mel and Deo were married and they sold the farm, moved to Redondo Beach and opened up the state's first dive shop.

Mel and Deo offered free dive lessons to anyone who bought equipment. Determined to develop the sport, Mel modified equipment and snorkel gear to make it easier to use. The Fishers also made some of the first underwater films, showing people the glories of the ocean. In around 1959, Mel began diving on shipwrecks and soon discovered a passion for historic salvage and treasure hunting.

Hearing of a treasure fleet from 1715 that sank off the coast of Florida, the Fishers decided to close the shop, move to Florida and look for treasure full time. Not too long into their search, they uncovered a carpet of gold coins on the seabed. This was the first of several breath-taking discoveries that spurred the pair on.

In 1968, Mel and Deo were looking for other places to dive, having found much of the 1715 fleet. It was then that a friend gave them a copy of Potter's 'The Treasure Diver's Guide', in which the Nuestra Senora de Atocha was described as one of the richest shipwrecks ever lost. And so, for Mel and Deo, the search was on.

Mel and his team searched the ocean bed every day for three years without finding anything from the Atocha. Then in 1971, one of the divers found a gold chain eight and a half feet long. Two years later, Mel's son Kane found a single sliver bar, with numbers inscribed on it that matched the manifest of the Atocha.

On July 13, 1975 - after seven years of searching - Mel's oldest son Dirk found five bronze cannons from the Atocha. Everyone thought that the 'motherlode' was close but, a week later, tragedy struck. One of their boats capsized during the night and Dirk, his wife Angel and diver Rick

Gage were all lost. In all, the hunt for the Atocha claimed four young lives, but the search continued.

Mel always believed they would find the treasure of the Atocha and he just kept going, becoming famous for his saying, "Today is the day." His perseverance was almost inhuman. He searched the ocean floor every day for more than a decade.

Mel Fisher epitomises what perseverance is all about. And it paid off for him. On July 20, 1985 - after nearly seventeen years of searching daily - a magnetometer contact indicated a large target on the seabed. Two divers went down to investigate and found they were sitting on an entire reef of silver bars. They had finally found the motherlode!

All in all, Mel Fisher and his team found 127,000 silver coins, more than 900 silver bars and 700 high quality emeralds, roughly 2,500 lighter stones, over 250 pounds of gold bars and hundreds of items of jewellery, silverware, crucifixes and gold coins.

Estimates put the wreck's value around $400 million. Mel Fisher had done it! With a total commitment and by persisting for years, he had realised his dream.

Adapted from various versions on the internet

CHAPTER NINETEEN : PRIORITIES

WALKING ON WATER...

One of the Dalai Lama's favourite stories is of a Zen disciple who left his village to live in the neighbouring forest and seek enlightenment.

He devoted himself to being able to walk on water. Finally, after many years of practice, the disciple mastered the technique.

Then one day, he saw his Zen Master walking by. Keen to demonstrate his mastery, the disciple leapt to his feet and proceeded to walk across the nearby river whilst his Master watched.

"How long did it take you to learn to walk on water?" asked the Zen Master.

"Twenty-seven years," the disciple replied, proudly.

"You idiot," the Zen Master said. "For a few pennies you could have taken the ferry."

Sometimes it's worth questioning what we're seeking to accomplish with our time on Earth, and if it's worth it. If it is, ask ourselves are we doing the right things to fulfil our desires?

A Zen parable

WHAT WILL MATTER

R eady or not, some day it will all come to an end.

There will be no more sunrises, no minutes, hours or days.

All the things you collected, whether treasured or forgotten, will pass to someone else.

Your wealth, fame and temporal power will shrivel to irrelevance.

It will not matter what you owned or what you were owed.

Your grudges, resentments, frustrations and jealousies will finally disappear.

So too, your hopes, ambitions, plans and to-do lists will expire.

The wins and losses that once seemed so important will fade away.

It won't matter where you came from or what side of the tracks you lived on at the end.

It won't matter whether you were beautiful or brilliant.

Even your gender and skin colour will be irrelevant.

So what will matter?

How will the value of your days be measured?

What will matter is not what you bought but what you built, not what you got but what you gave.

What will matter is not your success but your significance.

What will matter is not what you learned but what you taught.

What will matter is every act of integrity, compassion, courage, or sacrifice that enriched, empowered or encouraged others to emulate your example.

What will matter is not your competence but your character.

What will matter is not how many people you knew, but how many will feel a lasting loss when you're gone.

What will matter is not your memories but the memories that live in those who loved you.

What will matter is how long you will be remembered, by whom and for what.

Living a life that matters doesn't happen by accident.

It's not a matter of circumstance but of choice.

Choose to live a life that matters.

By Michael Josephson

FIRST THINGS FIRST, THE JAR OF LIFE

A philosophy professor stood before his class and had some items in front of him. When class began, without a word he picked up a large empty mayonnaise jar and proceeded to fill it with rocks right to the top, rocks about two inches in diameter.

He then asked the students if the jar was full. They agreed that it was.

So the professor then picked up a box of pebbles and poured them in to the jar. He shook the jar lightly. The pebbles, of course, rolled into the open areas between the rocks. The students laughed.

He asked his students again if the jar was full. They agreed that yes, it was.

The professor then picked up a box of sand and poured it into the jar. Of course, the sand filled up everything else.

"Now," said the professor, "I want you to recognise that this is your life. The rocks are the important things - your family, your partner, your health and your children - anything that is really important to you.

"The pebbles are the other things in life that matter, but on a smaller scale. The pebbles represent things like your job, your house, your car.

"The sand is everything else, the small stuff.

"If you put the sand or the pebbles into the jar first, there is no room for the rocks. The same goes for your life. If you spend all your energy and time on the small stuff, material things, you will never have room for the things that are truly most important.

"Pay attention to the things that are critical in your life. Play with your children. There will always be time to go to work, clean the house, give a dinner party and fix the garden. Take care of the rocks first - the things that really matter."

At the end of the professor's demonstration, one of the students took the jar (full of rocks, pebbles and sand) and added a full glass of water! The water was absorbed by the sand.

The Moral: whatever your life is filled with, there will always be some room left for more if you set your priorities first.

Author Unknown

■ ■ ■

FIVE MORE MINUTES

While at the park one day, a woman sat down next to a man on a bench near a playground. "That's my son over there," she said, pointing to a little boy in a red sweater who was gliding down the slide.

"He's a fine-looking boy", the man said. "That's my daughter on the bike in the white dress."

Then, looking at his watch, he called to his daughter. "What do you say we go, Melissa?"

Melissa pleaded, "Just five more minutes, Dad. Please? Just five more minutes." The man nodded and Melissa continued to ride her bike to her heart's content. Minutes passed and the father stood and called to his daughter again. "Time to go now?"

Again, Melissa pleaded, "Five more minutes, Dad. Just five more minutes." The man smiled and said, "OK."

"My, you certainly are a patient father," the woman responded.

The man smiled and then said, "Her older brother Tommy was killed by a drunk driver last year while he was riding his bike near here. I never spent much time with Tommy and now I'd give anything for just five more minutes with him. I've vowed not to make the same mistake with Melissa. She thinks she has five more minutes to ride her bike. The truth is, I get five more minutes to watch her play."

Author Unknown

THE DATE

After twenty-one years of marriage, my wife wanted me to take another woman out to dinner and a movie. She said, "I love you, but I know this other woman loves you and would love to spend some time with you."

The other woman my wife wanted me to take on a date was my mother, who had been a widow for nineteen years, but the demands of my work and my three children had made it possible to visit her only occasionally. That night, I called to invite her out for dinner and a movie and she asked, "What's wrong, are you ok?"

My mother is the type of woman that suspects that a late-night call or a surprise invitation is a sign of bad news. "I thought that it would be pleasant to spend some time with you, just the two of us," I responded. She thought about it for a moment, and then said, "I would like that very much."

That Friday after work, as I drove over to pick her up I was a bit nervous. When I arrived at her house, I noticed that she, too, seemed to be nervous about our date. She waited in the door with her coat on. She had curled her hair and was wearing the dress that she had worn to celebrate her last wedding anniversary. She smiled from a face that was as radiant as an angel. "I told my friends that I was going to go out with my son, and they were impressed," she said, as she got into the car. "They can't wait to hear about our date."

We went to a restaurant that, although not elegant, was very nice and cosy. My mother took my arm as if she were the First Lady. After we sat down, I had to read the menu. Her eyes could only read large print. Half way through our starter, I lifted my eyes and saw Mum sitting there staring at me. A nostalgic smile was on her lips. "It was me who used to have to read the menu to you when you were small," she said. "Then it's time that you relax and let me return the favour," I responded.

During the dinner, we had an agreeable conversation – nothing extraordinary but catching up on recent events of each other's life. We talked so much that we missed the movie. As we arrived at her house later, she said, "I'll go out with you again, but only if you let me invite you."

I agreed.

"How was your dinner date?" asked my wife when I got home. "Very nice, much more so than I could have imagined," I answered.

A few days later my mother died of a massive heart attack. It happened so suddenly that I didn't have a chance to do anything for her. Sometime later, I received an envelope with a copy of a restaurant receipt from the same place mother and I dined. An attached note said: "I paid this bill in advance. I wasn't sure that I could be there, but never less, I paid for two plates – one for you and the other for your wife. You will never know what that night meant for me. I love you, son."

At that moment, I understood the importance of saying in time: "I Love You" and giving our loved ones the time that they deserve.

Nothing in life is more important than your family. Give them the time that they deserve; these things cannot be put off till some other time.

Author Unknown

MAKE THE MOST OF TODAY

Imagine there is a bank that credits your account each morning with £86,400.

It carries over no balance from day to day. Every evening, it deletes whatever part of the balance you failed to use during the day. What would you do?

Draw out every penny, of course!!!

Each of us has such a bank. Its name is TIME.

Every morning, it credits you with 86,400 seconds.

Every night it writes off, as lost, whatever of this you have failed to invest to good purpose.

It carries over no balance.

It allows no overdraft.

Each day it opens a new account for you.

Each night it burns the remains of the day.

If you fail to use the day's deposits, the loss is yours.

There is no going back.

There is no drawing against the "tomorrow".

You must live in the present on today's deposits.

Invest it so you can withdraw the utmost in health, happiness, and success!

The clock is running. Make the most of today.

To realise the value of one year, ask a student who has failed his final exam.

To realise the value of one month, ask the parent of a premature baby.

To realise the value of one week, ask the editor of a weekly newspaper.

To realise the value of one day, ask a daily wage labourer who has a large family to feed.

To realise the value of one hour, ask the lovers who are waiting to meet.

To realise the value of one minute, ask a person who has missed the train, the bus or a plane.

To realise the value of one second, ask a person who just avoided an accident.

To realise the value of one millisecond, ask the person who has won a silver medal at the Olympics.

Keep in mind that time waits for no one. Make the most of today.

Author Unknown

COUNTING MARBLES

The older I get, the more I enjoy Saturday mornings. Perhaps it's the quiet solitude that comes with being the first to rise, or maybe it's the unbounded joy of not having to be at work. Either way, the first few hours of a Saturday morning are most enjoyable.

A few weeks ago, I was shuffling toward the kitchen, with a steaming cup of coffee in one hand and the morning paper in the other. What began as a typical Saturday morning turned into one of those lessons that life seems to hand you from time to time.

Let me tell you about it. I turned the volume up on my radio in order to listen to a Saturday morning talk show. I heard an older sounding chap with a golden voice. You know the kind; he sounded like he should be in the broadcasting business himself.

He was talking about "a thousand marbles" to someone named Tom. I was intrigued and sat down to listen to what he had to say. "Well, Tom, it sure sounds like you're busy with your job. I'm sure they pay you well but it's a shame you have to be away from home and your family so much. Hard to believe a young fellow should have to work sixty or seventy hours a week to make ends meet. Too bad you missed your daughter's dance recital." He continued, "Let me tell you something Tom, something that has helped me keep a good perspective on my own priorities." And that's when he began to explain his theory of 'a thousand marbles.'

"You see, I sat down one day and did a little arithmetic. The average person lives about seventy-five years. I know, some live more and some live less, but on average, folks live about seventy-five years. Now then, I multiplied seventy-five by fifty-two and I came up with 3,900 which is the number of Saturdays that the average person has in their entire lifetime.

"Now, stick with me, Tom, I'm getting to the important part. It took me until I was fifty-five years old to think about all this in any detail." He went on, "and by that time I had lived through more than 2,800 Saturdays. I got to thinking that if I lived to be seventy-five, I only had about a thousand of them left to enjoy. So I went to a toy store and bought every single marble they had. I ended up having to visit three toy stores to round-up 1,000 marbles. I took them home and put them inside a large, clear plastic container right here in my workshop next to the radio. Every Saturday since then, I take one marble out and throw away.

"I found that by watching the marbles diminish, I focused more on the really important things in life. There is nothing like watching your time here on this earth run out to help get your priorities straight. Now, let me tell you one last thing before I sign-off and take my lovely wife out for breakfast. This morning, I took the very last marble out of the container. I figure if I make it until next Saturday then God has blessed me with a little extra time to be with my loved ones...

"It was nice to talk to you Tom, I hope you spend more time with your loved ones, and I hope to meet you again someday. Have a good morning!"

You could have heard a pin drop when he finished. Even the show's moderator didn't have anything to say for a few moments. I guess he gave us all a lot to think about. I had planned to do some work that morning, and then go to the gym. Instead, I went upstairs and woke my wife up with a kiss. "C'mon honey, I'm taking you and the kids to breakfast." "What's brought this on?" she asked with a smile. "Oh, nothing special," I said. "It has just been a long time since we spent a Saturday together with the kids. Oh, and by the way, can we stop at a toy store while we're out? I need to buy some marbles."

Adapted from various versions on the internet

* * *

ONE MONTH TO LIVE

This Saturday evening had been fun. We had eaten pizza together, listened to some good music and now we all were sitting in the back yard of Laura's house. The summer was hot and many hours after the sunset it was still pleasantly warm.

We looked at Laura.

"What do you mean? One month to live? Why do you ask? Oh please, don't say that you..."

"No, no, no!" Laura laughed, "I'm perfectly healthy and all right. But my neighbour told me of a relative who went for a routine check-up with the doctor and suddenly heard he only had one month to live. Imagine! One month left!"

"Oh, how horrible..." We all felt compassion for the man.

"And so I began to think what I would do if I had only one month to live..." Laura said.

We sat there sipping home-made lemonade (Laura's speciality), and said nothing.

"Here," Laura took out a notepad and a pen. "Write down what you would do. Just out of curiosity."

We tried to protest, but Laura would not give up.

"No, seriously! Imagine how you would feel if you were told you only had one month to live. You would certainly want to do something important with the time you had left! What is it? Don't you want to know what you would really, really, want to do? Three things! We are always complaining how we would be happy, if only... So what are those things that would make you happy? The things you would absolutely want to do?"

Reluctantly, we took the notepad and pen and for a while nobody spoke. We all wrote something, tore the page and gave the notepad and pen to the next person. Then we looked at Laura. "Now what?"

She smiled. "Now - go out and do those things!"

We looked at her, speechless.

"Yes, don't you see? What did we talk about the whole evening? How we have time for nothing else but work, work, work all the time. Taking care of other people's needs, building other people's businesses. We all come home tired in the evenings and all we have energy for is to eat, do the laundry and flop on the sofa to watch TV.

249

What happened to the dreamers we all were at school? You, Mark, weren't you supposed to become an archaeologist? Our very own Indiana Jones?"

"Yes, but..."

"And Tina, you were supposed to set up a shop selling clothes you yourself made. What happened? How did you end up as an accountant? You had such talent!"

"Well, accounting pays the bills..."

"The bills...," Laura almost snorted. "It seems we all live only for the bills. Where are all our dreams? You want to hear what I wrote?"

We mumbled in agreement, a bit taken aback by her excitement.

"My three things to do if I had one month to live." Laura cleared her throat. "One: travel to Rome and sit on the Spanish steps toasting to life with champagne. Real champagne, mind you! Two: take all my photos and write stories about them. Who is who, what was good about them, and why the photo was taken. Three: sell my house and use the money to have the greatest funeral party ever - while I was still alive."

We nodded in agreement for the first two and laughed at the third. It sure sounded like Laura, that one. She loved throwing parties and inviting people over.

"Now, the rest of you."

We read what we had written. The things we would do if we had one month to live. Call all our family members and friends and tell them we loved them. Travel to Hawaii and watch the sun set. Go to see a real volcano. Write a novel. Go to the opera. Paint scenery we loved. Donate money to a charity. Buy a new car. Read the Bible from cover to cover. Go meditate in a Buddhist centre. Plant trees. Read that archaeology book that had been collecting dust for years.

When the last one of us had finished reading, Laura looked at us.

"Did you listen to what you just said? All those things are things you could do right now. So why don't you? Why have you built mental walls that stop you from living life as you would really want?"

We sat in the soft, warm night, with the stars twinkling above us, the soft wind caressing our cheeks and hair. No one said a thing. Then Laura got up.

"You know - I think I'll go check the travel agencies on the net and book myself a trip to Rome. Want to come along, Jim? I'm sure there are trips to Vesuvius or Etna being sold there too."

Mark got up too, following Laura and Jim.

"I'll come too. Maybe you can let me check archaeology courses when you've booked your trip."

They left and the rest of us looked at each other.

"I think I'll go buy some saplings tomorrow," Helen said.

"I'm sure I still can find my mother's Bible... I think Janet put it in a box in the attic...," Henry said.

For some reason, Karen had a leaflet about the local Buddhist centre in her pocket and now she was reading it. And I thought about all the notes I had made in order to write a novel. Yes, tomorrow I would start.

We have all lost loved ones. Family members, friends, neighbours.

It really makes you think, doesn't it?

Author Unknown

CHAPTER TWENTY :
VISION

FOLLOW YOUR DREAMS, NO MATTER WHAT

I have a friend named Monty Roberts who owns a horse ranch in San Ysidro, a district of San Diego, USA. He has let me use his house to put on fund-raising events to raise money for 'youth at risk' programs.

The last time I was there he introduced me by saying, "I want to tell you why I let Jack use my horse ranch. It all goes back to a story about a young man who was the son of an itinerant horse trainer who would go from stable to stable, race track to race track, farm to farm and ranch to ranch, training horses. As a result, the boy's high school career was continually interrupted. When he was a senior, he was asked to write a paper about what he wanted to be and do when he grew up.

"That night, he wrote a seven-page paper describing his goal of someday owning a horse ranch. He wrote about his dream in great detail and he even drew a picture of a 200-acre ranch, showing the location of all the buildings, the stables and the track. Then he drew a detailed floor plan for a 4,000-square-foot house that would sit on the 200-acre dream ranch.

"He put a great deal of his heart into the project and the next day he handed it in to his teacher. Two days later he received his paper back. On the front page was a large red F with a note that read, 'See me after class.'

"The boy with the dream went to see the teacher after class and asked, 'Why did I receive an F?'

"The teacher said: 'This is an unrealistic dream for a young boy like you. You have no money. You come from an itinerant family. You have no resources. Owning a horse ranch requires a lot of money. You have to buy the land. You have to pay for the original breeding stock and later you'll have to pay large stud fees. There's no way you could ever do it.' Then the teacher added, 'If you will rewrite this paper with a more realistic goal, I will reconsider your grade.'

"The boy went home and thought about it long and hard. He asked his father what he should do. His father said, 'Look, son, you have to make up your own mind on this. However, I think it is a very important decision for you.' Finally, after sitting with it for a week, the boy turned in the same paper, making no changes at all.

"He stated, 'You can keep the F and I'll keep my dream.'"

Monty then turned to the assembled group and said, "I tell you this story because you are sitting in my 4,000-square-foot house in the middle of my 200-acre horse ranch. I still have that school paper framed over the fireplace."

He added, "The best part of the story is that two summers ago that same schoolteacher brought 30 kids to camp out on my ranch for a week." When the teacher was leaving, he said, "Look, Monty, I can tell you this now. When I was your teacher, I was something of a dream stealer. During those years I stole a lot of kids' dreams. Fortunately, you had enough gumption not to give up on yours."

Author Unknown

THE BROOKLYN BRIDGE

In 1883, a creative engineer named John Roebling was inspired by an idea to build a spectacular bridge connecting New York with Long Island. However, bridge-building experts throughout the world thought that this was an impossible feat and told Roebling to forget the idea. It just could not be done. It was not practical. It had never been done before.

Roebling could not ignore the vision he had in his mind. He thought about it all the time and he knew, deep in his heart, that it could be done. He just had to share the dream with someone else. After much discussion and persuasion, he managed to convince his son Washington, an up-and-coming engineer, that the bridge could be built.

Working together for the first time, the father and son developed concepts of how it could be accomplished and how the obstacles could be overcome. With great excitement and inspiration, and the headiness of a wild challenge before them, they hired their crew and began to build their dream bridge.

The project started well, but when it was only a few months underway a tragic accident on the site took the life of John Roebling. Washington was also injured and left with a certain amount of brain damage, which resulted in him not being able to talk or walk.

"We told them so." "Crazy men and their crazy dreams." "It's foolish to chase wild visions."

Everyone had a negative comment to make and felt that the project should be scrapped, since the Roeblings were the only ones who knew how the bridge could be built.

In spite of his handicap, Washington was never discouraged; he still had a burning desire to complete the bridge and his mind was still as sharp as ever. He tried to inspire and pass on his enthusiasm to some of his friends, but they were too daunted by the task.

As he lay on his bed in his hospital room, the sunlight streamed through the windows. A gentle breeze blew the flimsy white curtains apart and he was able to see the sky and the tops of the trees outside, for just a moment.

It seemed that this was a message for him: don't give up. Suddenly, an idea hit him. All he could do was move one finger and he decided to make the best use of it. By moving this, he slowly developed a code of communication with his wife.

He touched his wife's arm with that finger, indicating to her that he wanted her to call the engineers again. Then he used the same method of tapping her arm to tell the engineers what to do. It seemed foolish, but the project was under way again.

For thirteen years Washington tapped out his instructions with his finger on his wife's arm, until the bridge was finally completed. Today, the spectacular Brooklyn Bridge stands in all its glory as a tribute to the triumph of one man's indomitable spirit and his determination not to be defeated by circumstances. It is also a tribute to the engineers and their teamwork, and to their faith in a man who was considered mad by half the world. It stands too as a tangible monument to the love and devotion of his wife, who for thirteen long years, patiently decoded the messages of her husband and told the engineers what to do.

Adapted from various versions on the internet.

■ ■ ■

ARNOLD SCHWARZENEGGER

The former Austrian-American bodybuilder has gone through many roles in his life, both on-screen and off. He started out as a penniless immigrant seeking the 'American dream' and ended up becoming an accomplished actor, author, politician and businessman.

But what do you really know about the life of the man behind the scenes? As Arnold puts it, "If my life was a movie, no one would believe it!"

Arnold Alois Schwarzenegger was born on July 30, 1947, into a strict Roman Catholic family in Thal, Austria. He grew up in a small village humbled by World War Two, living rather poorly in an old home with no plumbing, fridge or phone.

His mother would go from farm to farm, foraging for butter, sugar and grain. His father was a former Nazi and an abusive alcoholic who clearly favoured his eldest son, Meinhard. He nicknamed Arnold 'Cinderella', as he was the smaller and weaker sibling. Arnold was often beaten with a belt and berated for not being strong or smart enough.

Both Arnold and his brother followed a mandatory daily routine. They woke up at 6 am to do chores and earned their breakfast by doing sit-ups. After all chores and homework were done, their father sent them outside to practice soccer, even in the midst of a storm.

When Arnold was ten years old, he began dreaming of a better, brighter future in the Land of Opportunity. He watched newsreels about America and saw how happy and successful people were there. His discipline turned into drive. At school, he would tell his incredulous schoolmates, "I'm going to America."

Arnold's father wanted him to become a soccer player, so the boy trained religiously at a local club. But Arnold had his own ideas. He idolized a successful bodybuilder named Reg Park, who had won Mr. Universe, starred in movies and created a business empire in America. Arnold wanted that for himself - but he would have to go against what others wanted for him to discover his own path to success.

At thirteen, Arnold's soccer coach took the team to a local gym. The teen stared in awe at the weightlifting equipment and picked up his very first barbell. His mind was made up. If Reg Park could make it to America by working out, then so could he. He now had a plan for freedom: Bodybuilding, win Mr. Universe, go to America, make movies, then invest in business. Simple.

To his father's disappointment, Arnold dived headfirst into bodybuilding instead of soccer. He plastered pictures of strong men all over his room walls, prompting his mother to take him to a doctor, fearing he was gay.

But Arnold's focus was unbreakable. He trained obsessively, even breaking into a closed stadium on a Sunday to work out in the freezing cold. Every painful set and every extra rep was nothing but a step towards his goal.

At eighteen years old, Arnold Schwarzenegger enlisted in the Austrian Army to complete his mandatory year of service. He never stopped working towards his dream and even skipped his training to participate in the Junior Mr. Europe contest. He won the competition, but was promptly sent to military prison for going AWOL. It didn't matter to Arnold. He had won and was hungry for more.

Arnold came second in another bodybuilding contest and was later voted 'Best-Built Man of Europe', which pushed him into the spotlight. His heart was set on winning Mr. Universe, an opportunity he viewed as his ticket to America. So, as soon as his army service had ended, nineteen-year-old Arnold got on his very first plane and went to the Mr. Universe competition in London.

He didn't win, but one of the judges was so impressed with Arnold's physique that he offered to coach him. Arnold was broke, so he stayed in the judge's crowded family home above a gym. He trained tirelessly during the year leading up to the next Mr. Universe competition. At twenty, he became the youngest to win the title.

At only twenty-one, Arnold Schwarzenegger had already made a name for himself in the bodybuilding world, so his next move was to make films in America. He packed what little he had and landed in the place he had dreamed about since he was ten years old.

Arnold rapidly became a man of infinite ambition. He developed his brains along with his brawn, graduating from the University of Wisconsin with a major in International Marketing of Fitness and Business Administration.

At twenty-three, he became the youngest man ever to win 'Mr. Olympia', a record he still holds today. He won competition after competition, funnelling his earnings into business investments. Before he was even twenty-five years old, Arnold Schwarzenegger was a self-made millionaire.

When he decided to retire from bodybuilding, he was asked by a reporter what he would do next. Schwarzenegger smiled at him and calmly replied, "I'm going to be a movie star in Hollywood". "And how do you plan to make this dream come true?' the reporter asked. "The same way I became the most famous bodybuilder in the world. I will create a vision of who I want to be, and then I will start living like that person in my mind, as if it were already true."

However, his acting career didn't quite go as planned. Every agent and casting director would tell him his accent was too strong, his name was too long and his body was "too weird." Fortunately, his chiselled physique attracted the attention of Andy Warhol, who used Arnold as a model and later introduced him to big names in the film industry.

A few months later, Arnold landed a small role in the film 'Hercules in New York'. His English was terrible and he couldn't say his lines well enough, so production ended up dubbing him. But the role lit a fire under his dream of making it as a movie star. He went on to appear in increasingly bigger productions, eventually winning the 'New Star of the Year' awards at the Golden Globes for his role in 'Stay Hungry'.

At thirty years old, Arnold landed his breakthrough role in 'Conan the Barbarian'. The movie was a hit. It was followed by a sequel and then a string of action-hero movies including 'Commando', 'Total Recall', and, of course, 'The Terminator'.

Arnold Schwarzenegger was now globally recognised for his intense strength, deep voice and powerful body. His acting career was on the rise and his investments were blooming. Although entering politics was never his intention, in 1987 he married Maria Shriver, the niece of John F. Kennedy. He became more politically active in Republican circles.

During the early 1990s, Arnold chaired the President's Council on Physical Fitness and Sports and was also the ambassador of the Red Cross. In late 2003, Arnold ran for the Governor of California title, winning by a landslide. Nicknamed 'The Governator,' Arnold was an environmentally-conscious politician, who famously signed the first U.S. bill capping greenhouse gas emissions.

Arnold Schwarzenegger truly lives by one message: *'If you can see it, you can be it!'*

Adapted from various versions on the internet

AN OLD LADY'S POEM

What do you see, nurses, what do you see?
What are you thinking when you're looking at me?

A crabby old woman, not very wise,
Uncertain of habit, with faraway eyes?

Who dribbles her food and makes no reply
When you say in a loud voice, "I do wish you'd try!"

Who seems not to notice the things that you do,
And forever is losing a stocking or shoe.....

Who, resisting or not, lets you do as you will,
With bathing and feeding, the long day to fill....

Is that what you're thinking? Is that what you see?
Then open your eyes, nurse; you're not looking at me.

I'll tell you who I am as I sit here so still,
As I do at your bidding, as I eat at your will.

I'm a small child of ten ...with a father and mother,
Brothers and sisters, who love one another.

A young girl of sixteen, with wings on her feet,
Dreaming that soon now a lover she'll meet.

A bride soon at twenty - my heart gives a leap,
Remembering the vows that I promised to keep.

At twenty-five now, I have young of my own,
Who need me to guide and a secure happy home.

A woman of thirty, my young now grown fast,
Bound to each other with ties that should last.

At forty, my young sons have grown and are gone,
But my man's beside me to see I don't mourn.

At fifty once more, babies play round my knee,
Again, we know children, my loved one and me.

Dark days are upon me, my husband is dead;
I look at the future, I shudder with dread.

For my young are all rearing young of their own,
And I think of the years and the love that I've known.

I'm now an old woman ...and nature is cruel;
'Tis jest to make old age look like a fool.

The body, it crumbles, grace and vigor, depart,
There is now a stone where I once had a heart.

But inside this old carcass a young girl still dwells,
And now and again my battered heart swells.

I remember the joys, I remember the pain,
And I'm loving and living life over again.

I think of the years ... all too few, gone too fast,
And accept the stark fact that nothing can last.

So open your eyes, nurses, open and see,
...Not a crabby old woman; look closer ...see ME!!

When an old lady died in the geriatric ward of a small hospital near Dundee, Scotland, the nurses were going through her meagre possessions, and they found this poem. Its quality and content so impressed the staff that copies were made and distributed to every nurse in the hospital. One nurse took her copy to Ireland. The old lady's sole bequest to posterity has since appeared in the Christmas edition of the News Magazine of the Northern Ireland Association for Mental Health.

＊ ＊ ＊

THE DAFFODIL PRINCIPLE

Several times my daughter had telephoned to say, "Mother, you must come see the daffodils before they are over." I wanted to go, but it was a two-hour drive from Laguna to Lake Arrowhead.

"I will come next Tuesday," I promised, a little reluctantly, on her third call.

Next Tuesday dawned cold and rainy. Still, I had promised, and so I drove there. When I finally walked into Carolyn's house and hugged and greeted my grandchildren, I said, "Forget the daffodils, Carolyn! The road is invisible in the clouds and fog, and there is nothing in the world except you and these children that I want to see bad enough to drive another inch!"

My daughter smiled calmly and said, "We drive in this all the time, Mother."

"Well, you won't get me back on the road until it clears, and then I'm heading for home!" I assured her.

"I was hoping you'd take me over to the garage to pick up my car."

"How far will we have to drive?"

"Just a few blocks," Carolyn said. "I'll drive. I'm used to this."

After several minutes, I had to ask, "Where are we going? This isn't the way to the garage!"

"We're going to my garage the long way," Carolyn smiled, "by way of the daffodils."

"Carolyn," I said sternly, "please turn around."

"It's all right, Mother, I promise. You will never forgive yourself if you miss this experience."

After about twenty minutes, we turned onto a small gravel road and I saw a small church. On the far side of the church, I saw a hand-lettered sign that said, "Daffodil Garden."

We got out of the car and each took a child's hand, and I followed Carolyn down the path. Then, we turned a corner of the path, and I looked up and gasped. Before me lay the most glorious sight. It looked as though someone had taken a great vat of gold and poured it down over the mountain peak and slopes. The flowers were planted in majestic, swirling patterns - great ribbons and swaths of deep orange, white, lemon yellow, salmon pink, saffron and butter yellow. Each different-coloured variety was planted as a group so that it swirled and flowed like its own river with its own unique hue. There were five acres of flowers.

"But who has done this?" I asked Carolyn.

"It's just one woman," Carolyn answered. "She lives on the property. That's her home."

Carolyn pointed to a well-kept, A-frame house that looked small and modest in the midst of all that glory. We walked up to the house. On the patio, we saw a poster. "Answers to the Questions I Know You Are Asking", was the headline.

The first answer was a simple one."50,000 bulbs," it read. The second answer was, "One at a time, by one woman. Two hands, two feet, and very little brain." The third answer was, "Began in 1958."

There it was, The Daffodil Principle. For me, that moment was a life-changing experience. I thought of this woman whom I had never met, who, more than forty years before, had begun - one bulb at a time - to bring her vision of beauty and joy to an obscure mountain top. Still, just planting one bulb at a time, year after year, had changed the world. This unknown woman had forever changed the world in which she lived. She had created something of ineffable magnificence, beauty and inspiration.

The principle her daffodil garden taught is one of the greatest principles of celebration. That is, learning to move toward our goals and desires one step at a time - often just one baby-step at a time - and learning to love the doing, learning to use the accumulation of time. When we multiply tiny pieces of time with small increments of daily effort, we too will find we can accomplish magnificent things. We can change the world.

"It makes me sad in a way," I admitted to Carolyn. "What might I have accomplished if I had thought of a wonderful goal thirty-five or forty years ago and had worked away at it 'one bulb at a time' through all those years? Just think what I might have been able to achieve!"

My daughter summed up the message of the day in her usual direct way. "Start tomorrow," she said.

By Jaroldeen Asplund Edwards

● ● ●

FIFTY INTERESTING QUESTIONS

When you have a little spare time to think, review these interesting and thought-provoking questions:

1. If we learn from our mistakes, why are we always so afraid to make a mistake?

2. What is the difference between being alive and truly living?

3. Why do religions that support love cause so many wars?

4. Have you been the kind of friend that you would want as a friend?

5. Does love equal sex?

6. If happiness were the national currency, what kind of work would make you rich?

7. Are you doing what you believe in, or are you settling for what you are doing?

8. If the average human life span was 40 years, how would you live your life differently?

9. Are you more worried about doing things right, or doing the right things?

10. If you knew that everyone you know was going to die tomorrow, who would you visit today?

11. If you could offer a new-born child only one piece of advice, what would it be?

12. What one thing have you not done that you really want to do? What's holding you back?

13. Would you rather be a worried genius or a joyful simpleton?

14. Has your greatest fear ever come true?

15. Would you rather have less work to do, or more work you actually enjoy doing?

16. When was the last time you noticed the sound of your own breathing?

17. Decisions are being made right now. The question is: Are you making them for yourself, or are you letting others make them for you?

18. If you had all the money in the world but still had to have some kind of job, what would you choose to do?

19. When you're 90 years old, what will matter most to you?

20. This far in life, what is your biggest regret?

21. If you were at Heaven's gates, and God asked you "Why should I let you in?", what would you say?

22. What small thing could you do to make someone's day better?

23. What impact do you want to leave on the world?

24. When was the last time you tried something new?

25. What life lesson did you learn the hard way?

26. What do you wish you had spent more time doing five years ago?

27. What is the difference between living and existing?

28. If not now, then when?

29. Have you done anything lately worth remembering?

30. If you had to teach something, what would you teach?

31. What would you regret not fully doing, being or having in your life?

32. Is stealing to feed a starving child wrong?

33. What lifts your spirits when life gets you down?

34. Have you ever regretted something you did not say or do?

35. Why do we think of others the most when they're gone?

36. Is it more important to love or be loved?

37. If a doctor gave you five years to live, what would you try to accomplish?

38. Can there be happiness without sadness?

39. What's the one thing you'd like others to remember about you at the end of your life?

40. Is there such a thing as perfect?

41. What does it mean to be human?

42. Are you happy with yourself?

43. Can you think of a time when impossible became possible?

44. How do you spend the majority of your free time?

45. How have you helped someone else recently?

46. What did you learn recently that changed the way you live?

47. What is the nicest thing someone has ever done for you?

48. What will you never do?

49. In your lifetime, what have you done that hurt someone else?

50. When was the last time you were nice to someone and did NOT expect anything in return for it?

Author Unknown

■ ■ ■

THE FINAL DESTINATION

When I was seventeen, I read a quote that went something like: "If you live each day as if it was your last, someday you'll most certainly be right." It made an impression on me, and since then, for the past thirty-three years, I have looked in the mirror every morning and asked myself: "If today were the last day of my life, would I want to do what I am about to do today?" And whenever the answer has been "No" for too many days in a row, I know I need to change something.

Remembering that I'll be dead soon is the most important tool I've ever encountered to help me make the big choices in life. Because almost everything - all external expectations, all pride, all fear of embarrassment or failure - just fall away in the face of death, leaving only what is truly important. Remembering that you are going to die is the best way I know to avoid the trap of thinking you have something to lose. You are already naked. There is no reason not to follow your heart.

About a year ago, I was diagnosed with cancer. I had a scan at 7:30 in the morning, and it clearly showed a tumour on my pancreas. I didn't even know what a pancreas was. The doctors told me this was almost certainly a type of cancer that is incurable, and that I should expect to live no longer than three to six months. My doctor advised me to go home and get my affairs in order, which is doctor's code for prepare to die. It means try to tell your kids everything you thought you'd have the next 10 years to tell them in just a few months. It means to make sure everything is buttoned up so that it will be as easy as possible for your family. It means...say your goodbyes.

I lived with that diagnosis all day. Later that evening I had a biopsy, where they stuck an endoscope down my throat, through my stomach and into my intestines, put a needle into my pancreas and got a few cells from the tumour. I was sedated, but my wife, who was there, told me that when they viewed the cells under a microscope the doctors started crying because it turned out to be a very rare form of pancreatic cancer that is curable with surgery. I had the surgery and I'm fine now.

This was the closest I've been to facing death, and I hope it's the closest I get for a few more decades. Having lived through it, I can now say this to you with a bit more certainty than when death was a useful but purely intellectual concept:

No one wants to die. Even people who want to go to heaven don't want to die to get there. And yet death is the destination we all share. No one has ever escaped it. And that is as it should be, because Death is very likely the single best invention of Life. It is Life's change agent. It clears out the old to make way for the new. Right now, the new is you, but someday not too long from now, you will gradually become the old and be cleared away. Sorry to be so dramatic, but it is quite true.

Your time is limited, so don't waste it living someone else's life. Don't be trapped by dogma - living with the results of others' thinking - and don't let the noise of others' opinions drown out your own inner voice. Most importantly, have the courage to follow your heart and intuition; they somehow already know what you truly want to become. Everything else is secondary.

Steve Jobs (1955-2011) Chairman, CEO and Co-Founder of Apple Inc.

Stanford University address 2005, adapted from various versions on the internet

GRATITUDE

I am very grateful to so many people in my life:

My parents, Wilf and Rita;
thank you for your constant support, and for
instilling my love of books at an early age.

My children, Asa, Reannon and Lyle;
you are the wind beneath my wings.

My grandaughters, Lyla and Mya;
you remind me how to live in the now.

Carola, my partner;
thank you for your constant support.

To all my customer friends;
your support is why I write and read books.

Olivia;
thank you for proofreading,
editing and supporting this book.

Chris and Zara at Filament Publishing;
thank you for all you do.

A THANK YOU AND A REQUEST PLEASE!

Dear Reader,

Thank you for purchasing
Inspirational and Motivational Short Stories.

I hope the stories have inspired, moved and motivated
you as much as they did and still do for me.

Whenever I am in search of a good book, I tend to look at
the reviews (especially on Amazon) before I decide to
purchase. Unfortunately, less than 1% of consumers will
review a book they have read.

To most authors, reviews are like Gold Dust! Honest
reviews can help to spread the word for an author
like myself.

So, to help both myself and potential readers,
can you please leave me feedback on Amazon.

Thanks again for your support!

Barry Phillips